LET'S PLAY AND LEARN TOGETHER!

30 At-Home Activities for Infants and Toddlers

LET'S PLAY AND LEARN TOGETHER!

30 At-Home Activities for Infants and Toddlers

By Nancy Vogel and Christine Snyder

HIGHSCOPE®

Published by
HighScope® Press

A division of the
HighScope Educational Research Foundation
600 North River Street
Ypsilanti, Michigan 48198-2898
734.485.2000, FAX 734.485.0704

Orders: 800.40.PRESS; Fax: 800.442.4FAX; www.highscope.org
E-mail: *press@highscope.org*

Editor: Marcella Fecteau Weiner

Cover design, text, design, production: Kazuko Sacks, Profit Makers

Photography:
All photos are by Bob Foran with the following exceptions:
Andreas Gradin (Stocksy) — Front cover
Kevin McDonnell — 3, 41

Library of Congress Cataloging-in-Publication Data

Names: Vogel, Nancy, 1970- author. | Snyder, Christine M., 1981- author.
Title: Let's play and learn together! : 30 at-home activities for infants and toddlers / Nancy Vogel, Christine M. Snyder.
Description: Ypsilanti, MI : HighScope Educational Research Foundation, [2017]
Identifiers: LCCN 2016053482 | ISBN 9781573797597
Subjects: LCSH: Early childhood education--Activity programs. | Early childhood education--Parent participation. | Family recreation.
Classification: LCC LB1139.35.A37 V63 2017 | DDC 372.21--dc23 LC record available at https://lccn.loc.gov/2016053482

Printed in the United States of America

10 9 8 7 6 5 4 3 2

Contents

Introduction

As a teacher, you know that learning doesn't stop at the classroom door. You can use the activities in this book to help families become active learning partners with their infants and toddlers. Each activity has complete instructions and uses materials commonly found at home.

The Value of Parent and Family Engagement

Parents are children's first teachers and are therefore of key importance to their children's learning and development. Research has shown that parent and family engagement is critical to children's success in school, in terms of both academic achievement and social development. The importance of parent and family engagement is reflected in most early childhood program standards (Epstein & Hohmann, 2012). The activities in this book can help families extend their children's active learning throughout the day.

Active learning means children construct knowledge through their direct experiences with materials, ideas, events, and people.

Using This Book and CD

The activities in this book are organized under these categories:

- Art, Music, and Movement
- Communication, Language, and Literacy
- Early Math and Discovery
- Myself and Others
- Physical Development and Healthy Habits

To help you easily determine which age group each activity is for, look for the Infant or Toddler bar in the right-hand corner of each page.

Some activities include recipes and how-to instructions (e.g., how to make homemade play dough). All of these recipes and how-to instructions are also available at the back of this book so you can make copies to share with families.

The COR Advantage item addressed by each activity is given at the bottom of the first page of the activity. COR Advantage is the latest online version of the Child Observation Record (COR), which seamlessly integrates child assessment from birth through kindergarten. COR Advantage is aligned with the

Head Start Child Development and Early Learning Outcomes Framework; Common Core State Standards for kindergarten; state early learning standards; and the standards of national organizations in content areas such as literacy, mathematics, and science. It is integrated with the HighScope key developmental indicators (KDIs) at all age levels. The Infant-Toddler KDIs are guideposts for child development — the key learning experiences children need to engage with to learn and grow. Within each of six content areas, HighScope identifies the KDIs that are the building blocks of thinking and reasoning. Complete listings of the HighScope Infant-Toddler KDIs and COR Advantage items are given at the end of this book.

The CD packaged with this book contains all the activities shown on the book pages as well as the recipes and how-to instructions referred to in the activities. The owner of this book is authorized to photocopy book pages or to print activity pages from the CD for classroom use.

How the Activities Are Set Up

Each activity includes the following:

- Estimated cost
- A "mess factor" — that is, how much work will likely be needed to clean up after the activity
- Suggested location for the activity
- The developmental learning experiences children will have during the activity
- Materials needed
- Instructions for the beginning, middle, and end of the activity
- Suggestions for cleanup
- Suggestions for younger children (if applicable)
- Suggestions for older children
- Activity hints
- Activity extensions
- Strategies for accommodating children with special needs

Parts of an Activity

You can explain the basic parts of an activity to family members when giving them a copy of an activity from this book.

- At the **beginning** of the activity, the adult chooses a space appropriate for the activity, positions him- or herself and the child comfortably, offers the child materials (if applicable), and encourages the child to get started without waiting (if applicable).
- During the **middle** of the activity, the adult pays attention to the child's (or children's) actions and ideas. Note that children will often use the materials in unexpected ways. For example, a parent gave his two children chalk to use on the sidewalk outside. One child scribbled back and forth on the concrete. The other child watched the chalk roll down the drive, brought it back to the top, and rolled it down again.
- At the **end,** the adult gently brings the activity to a close. Adults can ease this transition by making a suggestion that keeps children active and gives them a sense of control, for example, by asking toddlers to help clean up the materials and/or to find a spot to display something they have made. For infants, adults will do most of the cleaning up while describing what they are doing as they clean up.

Working With Families

Strive to become an education partner with parents as a way to help foster children's learning. You can do this by establishing supportive relationships with families. In your interactions with family members, you can further encourage their participation with the following strategies:[1]

- Be open and approachable; listen to those parents willing and able to talk to you, and make it clear that you are available if they would like to make an appointment to speak with you separately.
- Help family members learn about their child's routine at your center.
- Encourage families to see value in each others' language and culture (e.g., host a "family day" and have a cultural potluck).

[1]Adapted from *Multicultural Programs,* by Tricia S. Kruse, with Polly Neill

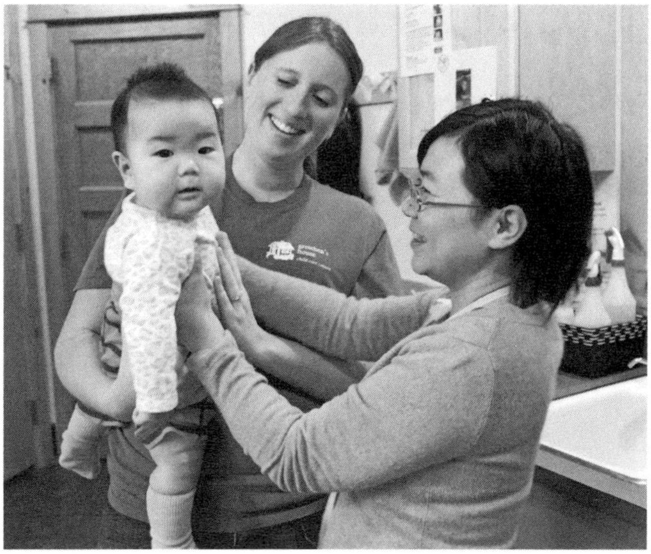

- Invite families to do a cooking activity during snacktime. Use this time to learn about food names and families' culture.
- Give workshops for family members, including workshops on child development.
- Invite parents into the classroom to observe or participate, or to visit during their lunch break. Let parents know they are welcome to call to check up on their child.
- Talk informally with family members at daily dropoff and pickup times.
- Schedule home visits.
- Offer CPR and first-aid classes to families.
- Share important information in print and online.
- Copy and distribute activities from this book to families, based on children's development and what you know about family interests, and offer support to parents as they try activities at home with their children.

Tips and Strategies for Families

In the remainder of this introduction, you will find six handouts listing tips and strategies that can help parents create supportive interactions with their child:

- Tips for Interacting With Your Child
- Strategies for Helping Your Child Become a Reader
- How to Read With Your Child
- Active Learning at Home Throughout the Day
- Tips for Singing With Your Baby or Toddler
- Tips for Including Toddlers in Self-Care Routines

The owner of this book may make photocopies of these pages to give to parents.

References

Epstein, A. S., & Hohmann, M. (2012). *The HighScope Preschool Curriculum.* Ypsilanti, MI: HighScope Press.

Kruse, T. S. (2006). *Multicultural programs.* Ypsilanti, MI: HighScope Press.

Tips for Interacting With Your Child

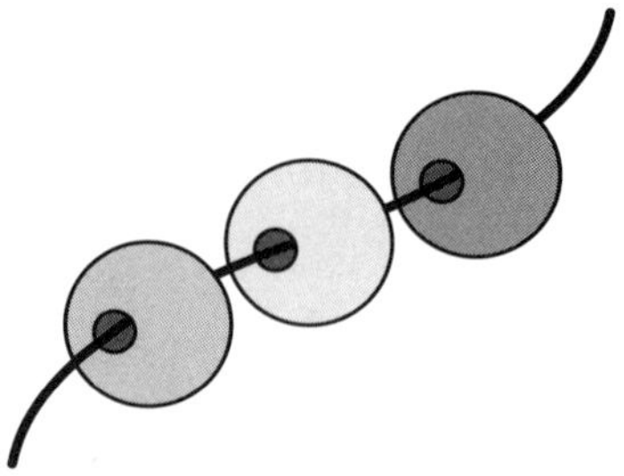

Young children are constantly learning — everything is new to them. Here are some adult-child interaction strategies that will help foster children's active learning and development.

- **Join children in their play.** Get on the floor with children, join them at a table or in the sandbox, play games with them — become engaged in what they are doing! Note that to get on an infant's or a toddler's level, you may need to be lying on your stomach.
- **Imitate what the children are doing; that is, play with the same materials in the same way as the children.** For example, an adult gives Emma a portion of play dough to explore. Emma squeezes the dough with both hands. The adult also squeezes the dough with both hands.
- **Make observations and comments about what you see the children doing.** While watching Emma squeeze the play dough, the adult comments, "You're squeezing the dough with both hands."
- **Ask open-ended questions, but ask them sparingly.** Open-ended questions encourage children to try out ideas, think, and talk, because these types of questions cannot be answered by a simple yes or no or a single-word response. Avoid questions that can be considered wrong or right. For example, instead of asking "What color is this ball?" ask "How could you make this ball move?" or "I wonder what you will do with this ball." Questions can help get a conversation going, but it is more important not to overwhelm a child with too many questions.
- **Follow children's pace and interests.** As you play with your children, follow their lead. For example, Holden was using farm animals and a barn. He made animal noises as he put the animals in the barn. He closed the barn doors and said, "All gone?" His dad sat next to him and commented, "Hmm, the animals were just here but now I can't see them! Where did they go?" Holden opened the doors and laughed.

Strategies for Helping Your Child Become a Reader

1. Have daily conversations with your child that model plenty of two-way interaction by pausing and acknowledging babbles or single words.
2. Keep a variety of printed materials and writing materials in your home.
3. Set up a special cozy reading space for your child with board books.
4. Let your child see you read and write.
5. Make reading with your child a daily experience and pleasurable habit.
6. Call your child's attention to reading and writing in everyday activities (e.g., in grocery lists or on simple road signs such as a stop sign). You can also identify single familiar letters, such as the first letter in your child's name on a cereal box.

7. Encourage your child to "read" and enjoy all the ways your child tries out reading, such as by turning pages, babbling, pointing to pictures, and naming objects in pictures.
8. Go to the library with your child.
9. Use television and technology wisely and keep the focus on active learning. Adult support and interaction during the use of educational programs on digital technology is essential for an active learning experience. Play the digital games with your child and extend learning by reinforcing concepts introduced in digital experiences by identifying letters in the child's environment, singing songs, and playing rhyming games throughout the day. For very young children, screen time should be limited (if used at all).

How to Read With Your Child

1. **Read slowly and naturally.** Pronounce the words carefully.
2. **Read with interest.** Make your voice expressive. If you are interested, your child will be too.
3. **Use different voices.** Give different voices or other qualities to the different characters in the story. Let your child come up with different voices.
4. **Pause in your reading and encourage your child to notice, point to, and name objects in the pictures; talk about the pictures, story, and characters.** Name the objects your child points to. Pose questions such as "I wonder what will happen next."

5. **Follow up on what you've just read.** Through regular daily activities, point out similarities between the objects, ideas, and feelings in the book and your child's experiences. Visit the kinds of places and do the kinds of things that appear in the book. Make up stories and play games that build on the book's ideas.

Active Learning at Home Throughout the Day

Just as children engage in active learning throughout the infant-toddler daily routine, parents can incorporate learning into different parts of the day at home. For example, you can do the following:

- Engage your child in early math experiences by having him or her help you match socks when you take the laundry out of the dryer.
- Name various items — fruit in the fruit bowl, toys on the shelf, or things they can see out the window.
- Foster early literacy experiences by making a grocery list together. Make a list using photos from the grocery store ads. This will allow children that are not yet reading to match items on the list to the items as you find them in the store. Older toddlers could cross off the pictures as you gather each item on your list.
- Name colors on packages when you do grocery shopping together.
- Sing songs through transitions between activities as opportunities for learning. For example, if children are playing in the living room and it's time to clean up before the evening meal, you might sing a song as you transition or allow your child to choose a song. Children can choose the way they move through the transition as you sing.
- Give your child a few plastic, metal, or wooden dishes and utensils to use while you cook a meal to pretend with.
- Have fun together!

Tips for Singing With Your Baby or Toddler

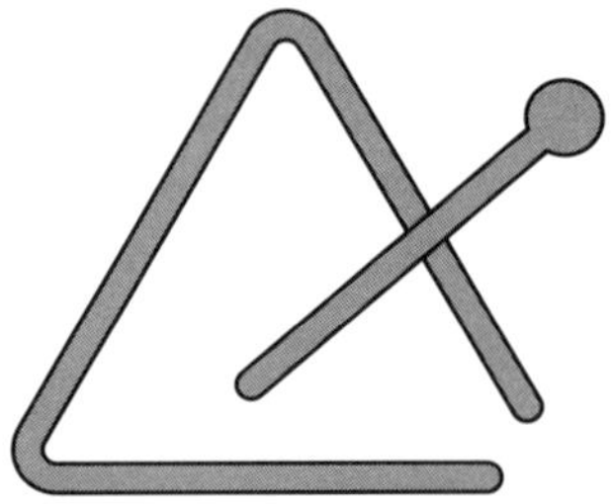

- **Physically connect with your child.** Holding your baby close in your arms (or in your lap) or making eye contact are all ways to physically connect with your baby while you are singing. This physical contact builds trust and attachment between you and your baby and increases the enjoyment he or she experiences in singing activities.
- **Sing slowly.** Sing the songs slowly to allow your child to hear the words and melody. When adults sing too fast, it is hard for children to hear and learn each word, making it more difficult for them to join in the singing.
- **Repeat the same songs often.** Repeating the songs you sing with your children increases their familiarity with the songs and makes it easier for them to learn the words and sing along.
- **Sing as a transition.** Singing during times when you have to move from one place or task to another can make the transition less stressful and more playful. Transitions can then become a playful time that you and your children look forward to, rather than a time of day that everyone dreads.
- **Sing to calm down.** Singing is a valuable strategy for preparing for rest times and calming unsettling feelings. Sing songs softly and slowly. Gentle rocking, back rubbing, or snuggling can add to the soothing experience.
- **Keep songs simple.** Choose songs that are repetitive and have simple melodies. If songs have many verses, sing one or two repeatedly (rather than singing all the verses) so that children can learn and get used to a limited number of words. Likewise, keep hand motions or gestures simple so children can copy them. Using a limited number of gestures and motions makes it easier for children to remember and copy them.
- **Share the songs you sing with other family members.** If there are particular songs that your child enjoys singing, be sure to let babysitters, grandparents, siblings, and other caregivers know which songs the child prefers. This enables family members to sing the child's favorite songs as well as increases the child's familiarity and enjoyment with those songs.

Tips for Including Toddlers in Self-Care Routines

- **Washing hands.** Minimizing the spread of germs and creating good habits are the adults' goals for hand washing. Children, on the other hand, are more interested in exploring the water, the soap, and their independence when washing their hands. Each time you help your children wash their hands, include a few seconds or minutes so they can explore the water and soap. When washing hands is a playful enjoyable experience, it will feel less like a required task that you have to remind children to do.
- **Brushing teeth.** It takes a lot of practice to learn how to brush teeth really well. Brush your children's teeth in front of a mirror so they can see what you are doing. As you brush your children's teeth, describe how you are moving the brush and name the parts of their mouth, for example, by saying "Now I'm brushing your front teeth, back and forth." Include time for children to move the brush around over their teeth using just water.
- **Getting dressed.** Invite your child to complete portions of the task of getting dressed and undressed such as pulling off socks, unstrapping shoes, pulling pants down, unzipping footie pajamas, and so forth. Periodically offer new simple tasks that they might be able to do.
- **Bathing/face washing.** Just like hand washing, children need time to explore the water and soap. In addition, offer children a small washcloth and remind them of places that need to be cleaned to include them in the process — even if you have to do some extra wiping at the end to get the spots they missed.

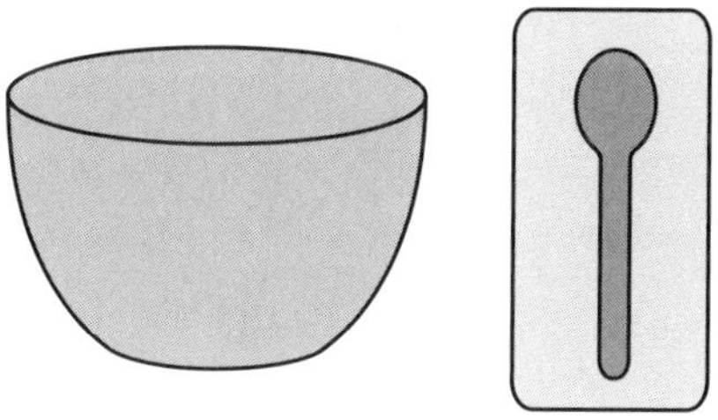

- **Eating.** While it can take practice and can be a little messy, offer children child-sized dishes and silverware so they can practice feeding themselves. Start with foods that are easier to control; for example, yogurt is easier to scoop and bring to your mouth in comparison to very runny soup. If a spill occurs, give the child a paper towel or a washcloth to help clean up the spill.
- **Toileting.** Learning to use the toilet happens at a different time for each child. Observe for your child's interest in using the toilet; offer chances to sit on the toilet; notice when your child has stayed dry between diaper changes; and if you are comfortable, let your child see you using the bathroom. Remain calm and positive through the toilet learning process, and remember that the "right time" for every child varies.

1 Art, Music, and Movement

Sing, Sing, Sing

Cost: None
Mess factor: None
Suggested location: Anywhere

Experiences your children will have

- Growing calm or becoming alert to sounds, tones, or music
- Responding to other people singing by joining in with vocalizations or motions

Materials

- Your voice and your children's voice

Beginning

Start this activity at any time (i.e., during your infant's alert moments or when having difficulty sleeping). Choose a song to sing based on your child's mood (a quiet lullaby if your child is upset or a song that is more upbeat).

Middle

If your infant is upset or trying to go to sleep, softly sing a lullaby or simply repeat his or her name and offer quiet words of assurance in a melodic way. Often, infants will stop crying, calm down, or fall asleep when they hear the soothing sound of a parent's or a familiar caregiver's voice.

If your infant is happy, sing a song that is more upbeat or one that includes movements and allows you to make up the words as you go along. For example, you could sing, "If You're Happy and You Know It" and adapt the lyrics as follows: "If you're happy and you know it, nibble Anna's toes..." or "If you're happy and you know it, kiss LeVar's tummy..." An older infant may "sing" with you or join in with some familiar hand or body movements. For example, you might sing and clap, "If you're happy and you know it, clap your hands," and your child might clap as well.

When introducing hand and body movements, think about your infant's developmental level and the milestones he or she has already reached, and customize the song to encourage what you know your child can do (e.g., if your child waves "bye-bye," include that as a verse of the song: "If you're happy and you know it, wave bye-bye"). Some other ideas (and you can think of some of your own as well) include: "Lift your arms," "Kick your feet," "Shake your head," "Pound the floor," and "Bounce up and down."

End

If your purpose in singing is to get your infant to sleep, the activity will end when your child (hopefully) falls asleep! If your infant has been alert during your song but begins to lose interest, you can end the song.

Cleanup

None

Older children

Toddlers who have been sung to as infants will build up a repertoire of songs that they enjoy singing or hearing you sing. They may request songs, using gestures or words, and also begin singing parts of familiar songs.

Hints

- Although there are mobiles, toys, books, and videos that play music, nothing can replace the soothing sound of your voice or the voice of another familiar adult. When you sing to your infant, there is an irreplaceable bond that is formed between you and your child. This is often accompanied by other interactions between you and your infant, such as establishing eye contact and sharing smiles.

More!

For older infants whose receptive language (language that they hear and understand) is more developed, sing something like "If you're happy and you know it, touch your tummy." Give your child time to think about where their tummy is and to respond to your request. If this seems too difficult, give a visual cue by pointing to your child's stomach and repeating the line in the song, giving your child another chance to touch their stomach. Repeat the song with different body parts if your child is enjoying the game.

Board books with lyrics to familiar songs as the text are another way to introduce songs to infants. As you flip through the books, *sing* the words to infants, rather than reading the words (the *Songs to Read* series by popular children's singer, Raffi, may be a good starting point).

Special needs accommodations

Infants with special needs typically respond in a positive way to songs and music; it encourages their language development and social interactions with others and may help relax tense muscles or calm feelings of anxiety. Make a habit of singing to your child frequently as music may continue to be an avenue for communication and learning throughout your child's life.

Shake It Up

Cost: Less than $5
Mess factor: None
Suggested location: Any comfortable space

Experiences your children will have

- Responding to sounds
- Creating sounds and music

Materials

Make several homemade shakers (see how-to instructions below).

Beginning

Bring your infant to a safe space, and tell them that you are going to explore sounds and shakers. Shake the shakers near your infant so they can see and hear them. If your child can hold objects, offer a shaker for them to use. Be sure to have a few shakers prepared, as your child may want to hold one in each hand.

Middle

Comment on your infant's reaction about the noise produced by the shaker. If your child can't yet hold items, describe the noise the shaker is making when you move it and repeat the sounds that he or she seems to enjoy (e.g., "Your eyes got really big when I shook the shaker"). If your child can hold items, describe how he or she is moving the shaker and the noise that is produced (e.g., "You're holding one shaker in each hand; one shaker makes a very loud noise and one makes a softer noise"). Your infant may enjoy mouthing the shaker, passing the shaker back and forth between hands, shaking one in each hand, and repeating these actions to continue to produce the same noises over and over.

Homemade Shakers

Choose a variety of different containers (that are empty and cleaned) for size, weight, and sound:

- Plastic eggs
- Plastic spice jars
- Formula bottles
- Plastic baby food containers
- Travel shampoo containers
- Water bottles (8 oz. size)

Fill each container with one of the following contents (choose one per container):

- Pea gravel
- Fish tank gravel
- Pennies
- Sand
- Beads
- Rice
- Dried beans
- Screws or nails

Securely seal the container with glue and/or tape.

End

As your infant begins to lose interest or you need to move on, let them know the activity is nearly over. If possible, allow your child to continue holding on to one of the shakers as you transition to the next part of your day.

Cleanup

Gather all the shakers into a basket or bag for use at another time.

Older children

Older children will enjoy "making music" with these shakers as well. Toddlers may enjoy walking, bouncing, or dancing while they use the shakers. Preschool children may enjoy helping you choose containers from around the house that could be made into shakers and filling them up before using them with your infant.

Hints

- To avoid the risk of choking hazards, be sure the shakers are securely sealed before offering them to your infant, and always be sure to use them with close supervision.

More!

Pay close attention to other sounds in the environment that your infant responds to with excitement and enjoyment. Older infants who are able to sit and manipulate objects may also enjoy banging on pots and pans with spoons or pounding their hands on upside-down laundry baskets, small storage containers, and empty coffee canisters.

Special needs accommodations

Infants vary in their ability to hold and manipulate objects. Before creating the shakers, determine what sizes, shapes, and weights of containers your infant can comfortably hold. Offer your child empty containers and observe which ones seem easiest to grasp and transfer between hands. For infants who cannot yet comfortably hold and manipulate objects, use the shakers where they can see and hear them.

Leader of the Band

Cost: None
Mess factor: None
Suggested location: A large, open space

Experiences your children will have

- Moving their bodies in various ways
- Initiating and copying movements

Materials

- Real instruments or homemade instruments

Ideas for Homemade Instruments

- Use recycled coffee cans, boxes with lids, oatmeal canisters, or small bowls or baskets as **drums** that children can bang on with their hands or with kitchen utensils (e.g., wooden spoons, spatulas).
- Put a few small items (e.g., beads, rocks) in a recycled plastic water or soda bottle and secure its cap to create **shakers.**
- Use metal bowls or pans that children tap on with whisks, spoons, plastic forks, or plastic combs for **chimes.**
- Give children two metal lids or two metal pie tins to use as **cymbals.**

Beginning

Tell your toddler that today you will be making some music. Offer him or her a couple instruments to try out. After your child has chosen one, select one for yourself.

Middle

Encourage your toddler to make music with the instrument in various ways. Copy your child's actions with your instrument, and describe what you are doing to help your child's awareness of and confidence in his or her ideas. Model another way to play the instrument (e.g., fast, slow, quietly), and describe what you are doing (e.g., "You're tapping yours really fast; I'm going to try tapping mine slowly"). This helps children think about new and different ways to use their bodies and materials. After some time playing with the instrument, invite your child to make a parade around the room or other open space. Allow your child to be the leader and choose where to go.

End

Let your child know that there is time for one more lap around the room (or space) before you need to move on to the next part of your day.

Cleanup

Gather up all the instruments to be used at another time.

Younger children

Carry nonmobile children in your arms or in a sling or carrier. Encourage mobile children to join in a parade by crawling or scooting along (try to move at a slow pace so they can keep up). Draw children's attention to the music being made, and comment on their reactions to the sounds. If your child can hold an object, offer him or her a shaker. For children that can sit independently, place a drum on the floor where they can reach it to bang on.

Older children

Older children enjoy playing instruments and marching in a parade too. Let them have a turn leading, and be sure they take turns following your toddler as well. Older children can also assist in making instruments before the activity.

Hints

- Children can be easily overstimulated when there is too much going on. To minimize overstimulation, only offer two types of instruments to start. Although there may be more than two instruments being played, there will be only two different sounds being produced, which can be less overwhelming. In addition, consider having children playing an instrument and staying in one place or marching around the room without an instrument (playing an instrument and moving around the room requires children to do two things at once). Accept the level and amount of engagement that your child is comfortable with.

More!

This activity can also be done outside (especially if your children are sensitive to noise), which will give them more space for making loud noises and marching around.

Special needs accommodations

Using one material in each hand may be challenging for some children. Offer to hold the large piece of an instrument (such as the coffee container or metal pan), and let your children bang on it with their hands or with a tool. You might need to stay in one place while your children focus on coordinating movements and repeating the action to make the sound.

Rub-a-Dub-Dub, Artist in the Tub

Cost: About $5
Mess factor: Minimal (contained in bathtub or bathroom sink)
Suggested location: Bathtub or bathroom sink (a white or light-colored sink or tub is best so the color will show)

Experiences your children will have

- Mixing colors
- Noticing color change in the water

Materials

- 2–4 small spray bottles or empty soap dispensers
- Food coloring or liquid watercolor
- Towels (for cleaning up and drying off)

Before you get started: Prepare the materials beforehand by filling the bottles or soap dispensers with water and adding a few drops of color to each.

Beginning

This activity can be done leaning over the bathtub or sink or in the tub. Fill the sink/tub with a small amount of lukewarm water. Offer your toddler the spray bottles or soap dispensers filled with colored water, and invite them to spray or pump water into the sink/tub. **Be sure to always closely supervise children using water.**

Middle

Give your toddler time to explore the bottle and figure out how to squeeze the lever to make the water come out. If your child becomes frustrated, gently offer to show them how to squeeze it (your child might need to use two hands). As your child sprays water on to the walls of the tub or sink, comment on the colors and describe how the colors drip down the wall and what happens when the colors mix. Join in the play by grabbing another bottle/dispenser and adding to the colors on the wall. Be sure to trade and swap bottles if your child makes that request.

End

Let your toddler know it is almost time to clean up and dry off, and give them a specific choice (e.g., "It is almost time to clean up and dry off. You have time to do two more sprays or three more sprays"). Count the sprays together and remind your child when he or she makes a final spray.

Cleanup

Dry your child off, and then wipe up any water that may have splashed on to the floor. Dump and rinse the bottles/dispensers and store them for use again at another time. Rinse the bathtub/sink to wash away any lingering colors.

Younger children

While they may not be able to squeeze spray bottles or pump the soap dispensers, younger children will enjoy splashing around in the water. Offer them scoops, cups, or funnels so they can explore filling and dumping the water.

Older children

Older children also enjoy exploring and mixing the color water and may be able to assist in preparing the bottles/dispensers. Prompt color mixing by saying something like "I wonder what would happen if we sprayed my color and your color at the same spot. What would the color look like then?" They could also mix colors using other materials, such as eye droppers or turkey basters.

Hints

- Place rugs and/or towels around the edge of the bathtub to minimize the possibility of slipping and lessen concern over the floor getting messy.

More!

Use spray bottles/soap dispensers with colored water outside on wooden fences, in the snow, or on pavement. Children will have more space to explore the colors and notice how they are mixing and blending together.

Special needs accommodations

Spray bottles and soap dispensers can be challenging for children to use while they are still developing strength in and control of their hands and fingers. Alternatively, you can use squeezable bottles (e.g., recycled, washed ketchup or salad dressing bottles) with colored water. Even if children aren't able to squeeze the water out, they can tip the bottle upside down and watch a slow stream of colored water trickle out. Or try bins or pitchers of colored water that children can scoop and mix or use a large paintbrush to dip in to paint the tub/sink.

Sing-along

Cost: None
Mess factor: None
Suggested location: Anywhere

Experiences your children will have

- Listening to and singing along with familiar songs
- Exploring vocal pitch

Materials

- None

Beginning

Start by singing a familiar song, and tell your toddler that you're going to be singing some different songs too.

Middle

Choose another song to sing that reflects your toddler's interests (e.g., if your child likes animals, sing "Old McDonald Had a Farm"). Keep the songs simple by singing only one verse and saving the hand motions or actions until your child has heard the words and melody several times.

After you have sung a song a few times, add in some motions/actions. Practice the motions first (limit motions to two or three per song to begin with), and encourage your toddler to copy before adding the words. You can add in more motions once your child is familiar with the words and original motions or actions.

Accept your child's level of participation, whether he or she is simply observing, trying out some of the actions, or singing some of the words. As you continue to sing the songs over time, you will notice your toddler joining in more each time; you may even overhear your child singing the songs at other times of the day. Suggested songs include "Old McDonald Had a Farm," "Row, Row, Row Your Boat," "Open, Shut Them," "Wheels on the Bus," and "Five Little Monkeys."

End

As your toddler begins to lose interest or if you need to move on, tell them that you have time to sing one more song. Let your child choose the song; if they can't tell you a song, choose one for them.

Cleanup

None

Younger children

Invite younger children close to where you are singing so they can hear your voice and watch the way you move. Observe how they respond to your singing (e.g., gaze at you intently, clap their hands, or make sounds with their mouths). Comment on their attempts to sing and move along with you.

Older children

Invite older children to sing along with you. They may enjoy choosing the song, coming up with unique rhymes, or adding additional movements.

Hints

- Sing slowly! Your children are still learning the words and how to form sounds with their mouths and control the pitch of their voices. When you sing slowly, they can watch how your mouth moves and hear each word so they can learn them and sing-along too!

More!

For songs that you sing often, make a "song card" for each song and put them in a recipe box or on a ring where your child can look at them and choose songs to sing. To make a song card, choose a note card that your child can easily hold. On the card, draw a symbol or cut out and paste a picture from a magazine that your child can easily understand. For example, for "Old McDonald Had a Farm," draw or use a picture of a barn or farm animals. On the flip side of the card, write down the words if the song is relatively new to you or if it would help other family members know the words to the song. Older children can help make the song cards too.

Special needs accommodations

For children with speech and language delays, move close to them so they can hear all the sounds and watch your mouth move. Be sure to annunciate your words clearly. Allow time for them to sing along, and expect that they may prefer to listen and watch you first or may only be able to sing a few words to start with. Repetition gives all children familiar and enjoyable practice. Choosing songs with rhyming (words with the same ending sounds such as *house* and *mouse*) and alliteration (words with the same beginning sounds such as *pease* and *porridge*) gives children practice producing similar sounds in different ways.

No-Worry Painting

Cost: Less than $15
Mess factor: Some
Suggested location: Outside

Experiences your children will have

- Exploring art materials
- Using art materials to make discrete marks

Materials

- Child-sized easel (optional — see "Hints" on the next page)
- Chubby paintbrushes
- Washable (nontoxic) paints
- Paper
- Paper/plastic cups
- Damp wash cloths or towels and a bucket of warm water

Before you get started: Set up a child-sized easel outdoors on a flat surface. Pour a small amount of paint into two cups, place one cup on the easel tray, and put the other one to the side for later. Attach a piece of paper to the easel. Fill up a bucket with water and gather some towels so you are ready for cleanup.

Beginning

Dress yourself and your toddler in playclothes. Show your child how to dip the paintbrush into the paint cup and brush the paint onto the paper.

Middle

If your toddler is more interested in exploring just the paint let your child use their fingers to paint on paper.

Older toddlers may try using a paintbrush but will need practice. As they learn how to control the paintbrush, they'll begin to make discrete marks on the paper and may notice that making different movements with their arms produces different lines and marks. Describe your child's movements while talking about the marks created.

End

Before ending the activity, try introducing a new color of paint or another paintbrush. If you've introduced two primary colors, talk to your child about how the colors change.

Cleanup

Leave artwork on the easel to dry or lay (and secure) the papers on the ground. Your toddler can help you throw away the paint cups and place the paintbrushes in clean water. Depending on how your child explored the paint, cleanup may be as simple as using some damp cloths or it might involve carrying your child directly into the bathtub!

Younger children

Infants' first experiences with art come from the different colors and textures adults offer them through visual stimulation, toys, and other objects (e.g., mobiles). Other objects offer infants a variety of textures to experience: a soft blanket on their bare legs, fresh blades of grass on their hands or feet, or the rough feel of tree bark on their fingertips.

Older children

Older children may begin making simple representations of such things as a tree or a house. As children develop, they will add more details and create more complex representations (e.g., a picture of the pet dog). Offer older children more paint colors, provide additional brushes, and talk to them about their paintings.

Hints

- For children who are beginning walkers or aren't used to standing for long periods of time, place paper on the ground and secure it with heavy rocks or tape (instead of using an easel).

More!

Purchase or make your own bathtub paints, and let your toddlers paint with a brush or finger on the tub. Since there won't be any artwork to save, take pictures.

Homemade Bath Paint

Materials

- ¼ cup tear-free baby wash or shampoo
- ¼ cup corn starch
- 1–2 tbsp. water
- 3–4 drops of food coloring

Directions

Combine cornstarch, shampoo, and food coloring. Add water until the mixture reaches the desired consistency. If it gets too runny, add more cornstarch; if it gets too thick, add more water. Store paint in small plastic containers (with lids).

Special needs accommodations

Children who are sensitive to textures or smells might be hesitant to use paint. If this is the case, try painting with water (children can compare the contrast of wet and dry surfaces) or introducing bathtub paints. Finger painting may be a good option for toddlers who have motor delays as it gives them the experience of exploring the paint with success, without the challenge of controlling a paintbrush.

2 Communication, Language, and Literacy

Beginning With Books

Cost: Less than $10 per book
Mess factor: None
Suggested location: A cozy spot

Experiences your children will have

- Touching, grasping, or mouthing books
- Turning the pages of books

Materials

- Board books with bright pictures, vivid photos, and interesting textures

Beginning

Find a cozy place to sit, position your infant comfortably on your lap, and introduce a book. With an older infant, offer a couple of books and ask which one he or she wants to read (depending on your child's level of understanding, they may — or may not — choose a book). Have several other books nearby to keep your reading time uninterrupted.

Middle

Give your child time to handle the book before you open it up. Infants may grasp it, turn it over, open and close it, drop it on the floor, or put it in their mouth, which are all normal behaviors and necessary steps in their book learning. In fact, you could make the process of *exploring* the book an activity (without even reading the book to your child). If you'd like to read the book, let your child continue exploring the book while you choose another book to read.

As you look at a book together, slowly read the words or simply talk about the pictures (let your child hold the book if he or she wants to). If there are things to feel, guide your child's hand to the interesting textures on the pages and describe each texture. Older infants may explore textures in a book independently (without needing your guidance) and may spend more time looking at the pictures or "talking" by babbling or saying simple words. When you and your infant are ready to move on to the next page, encourage your child to help you turn the page.

Note: When infants explore books independently, they may hold the book upside down. At this developmental stage, infants are not as concerned with looking at the pictures as they are with the *process* of looking through a book and turning the pages. As infants have more experiences with books, they will become more interested in looking at the pictures and will hold the book right-side up.

End

If your child begins to lose interest, close the book and put it down.

Cleanup

Infants who can grasp objects may be able to help you clean up by picking up the books and dropping them into a basket or box.

Older children

Older children may look at books right-side up, open them at the beginning, and turn the pages one at a time. As their speech develops, children will use phrases and sentences to talk about what is pictured in books.

Hints

- To make turning pages of a board book easier for infants, stick an adhesive dot of Velcro or felt on the top or bottom right-hand corner of each page. This creates more space between pages so that they are easier to grab hold of and turn.
- Keep in mind that lift-the-flap books and books with moving parts may not hold up well in the curious hands and mouths of infants.
- Infants may enjoy the novelty of books with battery-powered sound effects at first, but when the battery wears down, you'll need to replace it with a new battery, which often costs more than the original price of the book. Instead of spending your money on these types of books, purchase books with bold, interesting pictures or textures and create the sound effects yourself.

More!

To make your own textured board book, gather items that have different textures (e.g., scraps of cloth such as felt, satin, or velvet; fabric tassels, trims, and fringe; a piece of sandpaper). Cut square sheets of heavy card stock, paper, or cardboard into pieces about 6" x 6" (or whatever size you prefer) and then cut scraps of cloth and other textured items into pieces that will fit onto each page. Secure the items onto pages with glue, leaving enough room on the left side of each page for holes and fasteners. Punch two or three holes on the left side of each page (be sure the holes on each page line up with each other), and use ribbons to secure the pages.

Special needs accommodations

Infants who have visual impairments will enjoy books with interesting textures. Talk about the textures your child is touching as you guide their hands through the book's pages. Infants with developmental delays will explore books in many of the ways described here but may need more assistance with placing their hands on the various textures or with turning the pages.

Listen Up!

Cost: None
Mess factor: None
Suggested location: Anywhere

Experiences your children will have

- Responding to your voice in a variety of ways
- Responding nonverbally to simple statements or requests

Materials

- None

Beginning

Place younger infants on their back on a blanket on the floor, a changing table, or a bed. Older infants can sit independently (on the floor or in another place).

Middle

If your infant is lying on their back, begin talking by saying something like "It feels good to stretch out on your back and kick your legs!" Model conversation patterns by pausing in between sentences, which gives your infant time to explore your facial expressions, process your words and the inflection of your voice, and conjure up a response. Your child may respond to your voice by establishing eye contact, smiling, or cooing.

Try moving to the opposite side from which your child is looking and say your child's name to see if he or she responds. Make a game of it, and move to the other side of your infant to see if your child moves their head to find your voice.

If you give infants frequent opportunities to hear language (called *receptive* language), they will begin to understand some of your words. Try playing a game by saying something like "I'm going to touch your nose!" and then pause. If your infant doesn't respond (by wrinkling or touching their nose), touch their nose and say "I found your nose!" If your infant does touch their nose, you'll know that he or she understands and is ready to continue playing (i.e., by replacing "nose" with "toes").

End

Younger infants will give you cues that they are growing tired of this activity by beginning to cry, squirming on the floor, or arching their back. Older infants will also give you cues (e.g., may look away) when they are finished playing the game.

Older children

Toddlers can respond to simple statements and requests with words, connect their own experiences to the conversation, and respond in more of a give-and-take manner. Continue to give your children opportunities to listen to you speak; as they grow and develop, enjoy listening to their new vocabulary and ideas.

Hints

- Infants learn language through natural interactions with you and their environment. Avoid bombarding them with too many questions; instead, ask meaningful questions, for example, "Are you ready to go outside and swing?" Before they can respond verbally to your questions, infants will show that they understand you by gesturing, signing, pointing, or shaking their head "Yes" or "No."
- Decoding language is a major developmental milestone for infants. As infants continue to develop, they will begin to understand and respond to your simple statements or requests (e.g., a child might crawl over to pick up their "blankie" when told, "It's time to go to night-night"). Encourage infants' increased understanding of language by acknowledging their response (e.g., you might say, "You found your blankie; you're ready for bed. We'll go rock for a few minutes, and then I'll put you in your crib").

More!

Talk to infants throughout your daily activities. For example, you might say, "It's time to put on your pants. I need your leg. Let's put your leg through. Where are your toes? There they are!"

Talk about what your child is experiencing when you go for a walk in the neighborhood. You might say, for example, "I hear the birds chirping" or "The sun feels warm on your legs." Immerse your child in language, and don't shy away from using interesting words and vocabulary. As you speak, remember to pause in a natural, conversational pattern after each sentence, giving your child time to process your words and verbally or nonverbally respond. Your child won't understand everything you are saying but will eventually learn language by hearing it modeled.

Special needs accommodations

If you find that your infant frequently doesn't respond to your voice, speak to your pediatrician about your concerns. If your infant has a diagnosed hearing impairment or a developmental delay, be sure that your infant can see your face and your hands when you speak. Communicate with your infant using words, facial expressions, simple gestures, and signs for frequently used words. Also, be sure to reduce or eliminate the many kinds of background noise and speak slowly and clearly.

Talk to Me, Baby

Cost: None
Mess factor: None
Suggested location: Anywhere

Experiences your children will have

- Making verbal sounds, such as cooing and babbling
- Saying or signing a single word

Materials

- Infant toys with bright colors, stimulating patterns, interesting textures, and soothing sounds (e.g., soft toys with crinkly materials, ribbons, and rattles attached; teething rings; plastic keys; stuffed animals)

Beginning

Notice when your infant makes attempts at speech at times when he or she is content, set aside all distractions, and get ready to have a "conversation"!

Middle

When your infant begins cooing, respond by imitating your child's vocalizations or by talking (e.g., you might say, "You have a lot to say. Will you tell me some more stories?"). Model conversation patterns by pausing occasionally so your child has time to explore your facial expressions, think about what they will do next, and conjure up a response. When your child uses inflections while cooing, respond to their changes in vocalization.

Older infants may soon begin babbling, which sounds more like speech. When your child begins to make these sounds, repeat and then introduce new sounds. For example, if your child makes the /m/ sound, face your infant and repeat the /m/ sound over and over: "Ma, ma, ma, ma." You may want to introduce a new sound, /b/; repeat the new sound, saying "Ba, ba, ba, ba"; and give your child a chance to respond. Even if children aren't quite ready to imitate a newly introduced sound, they will make new sounds in the coming months as their speech develops.

You may also want to introduce a few simple signs for frequently used words, such as *more, all done, eat,* or *drink* (look up American Sign Language [ASL] websites to find these simple signs.) Just as your child won't begin repeating words right away, they won't imitate signs right away either; your child needs time to see, hear, and practice using the signs. You may find, however, that infants will sign some of these common words well before they are able to say them.

As your child develops, they will start saying a few simple words, which may include words that only you or your child's other primary caregivers understand. Encourage your infant's early attempts at speech by clearly repeating the word(s) they say. Introduce your child to new vocabulary by talking about what you see, hear, feel, and smell when taking walks and reading books with interesting photos.

End

Depending on your child's age and attention span, they may grow tired of "talking" to you. Follow your child's cues, move on to a new toy or a different part of your daily routine, and know that the conversation you shared with your child was an important step in their speech and language development.

Cleanup

None

Older children

Encourage toddlers' speech and language development by talking to them and introducing new vocabulary as you and your children play, experience daily activities, and respond to emotions. Read to your older children frequently.

Hints

- Set aside or turn off distractions (e.g., computer, phone, television) when your children are talking to you so that you can develop the habit of giving your children undivided attention when they speak to you.
- If you're interested in using simple hand signs with your child, introduce them into conversations, rather than using flash cards or drill-and-practice tactics.

More!

Sing songs with your child. Consider singing "Old MacDonald" when your child is learning to make new sounds; repetition of sounds in phrases (e.g., "With a baa-baa here and a baa-baa there") can encourage babbling infants to practice new sounds and older infants may be able to imitate certain sounds and words.

Special needs accommodations

Infants who have developmental delays or hearing impairments may need more time to reach particular speech and language milestones. Consider modeling signs for frequently used words as you talk to your child and then add to your child's signing vocabulary as their understanding increases. Some infants may be able to communicate by signing words before they can speak words, which may keep them from feeling frustrated in their attempts to communicate.

Rhyme Time

Cost: None
Mess factor: None
Suggested location: Anywhere

Experiences your children will have

- Hearing words that rhyme
- Repeating rhyming words and nursery rhymes

Materials

- None

Beginning

Rhyming (words with the same ending sound, e.g., *clock* and *dock*) is an important element of learning how to read and sound out words. Playful experiences with rhyming can increase your child's enjoyment and ability to remember new vocabulary and rhyming sounds. To start this activity, let your child know that you will be saying and singing nursery rhymes. Some suggested rhymes to start with include "Hickory, Dickory, Dock," "Row, Row, Row Your Boat," "Baa, Baa Black Sheep," "Little Miss Muffet," "Rub-a-Dub-Dub," and "Jack and Jill."

Middle

As you say the rhymes, place emphasis on the rhyming words: "Hickory, dickory, **dock.** The mouse ran up the **clock.**" After you finish the rhyme, point out the words that rhymed: "*Dock* and *clock*; those words rhyme!" Drawing children's attention to the rhyming words also helps them catch on to the cadence or rhythm of the rhyme. Repeat each rhyme several times so your child can learn all the words in the rhyme and specifically hear the rhyming words you emphasize. Children may request that you repeat the entire rhyme again, a few words from the rhyme, or the rhyming words. Repetition is important to build familiarity, support interest, and give children an opportunity to join in and spontaneously say rhymes. Acknowledge both common rhyming words and nonsense rhyming words.

End

As your toddler begins to lose interest or you need to move on, let your child know that there is time to say one more rhyme. Ask your child to choose the last rhyme. If your child is nonverbal, choose a rhyme they seemed to like.

Cleanup

None

Younger children

While they may not notice, respond to, or repeat the rhyming words, younger children benefit from hearing the rhyming words and may enjoy clapping or bouncing along to the rhythm. To support their feeling of the beat, you can bounce them on your knee or pat their back to the beat.

Older children

To engage older children, ask them to think of other nursery rhymes or songs that have rhyming words. Encourage them to clap or tap out the beat. As an extension, encourage older children to hunt around for objects in the environment that rhyme (e.g., *skirt, shirt*; *book, hook*). Older children may enjoy making up nonsense rhyming words too!

Hints

- Rest assured that even if your children aren't repeating the rhyming words, they are hearing them and starting to add those words to their vocabulary. It is quite common for children to repeat songs and nursery rhymes a few days (or even a few weeks) after they have experienced them. Likewise, you may notice your children singing or saying rhyming words when they think you can't hear them (e.g., when they are in bed or are in their car seat).

More!

Throughout the day, point out times when your child rhymes spontaneously or when objects near each other rhyme. For example, you might say, "You just said *blue* and *shoe*. Those words rhyme!" or "Your brown bear is sitting in the chair. *Bear* and *chair* — that's a rhyme!"

Special needs accommodations

Nonverbal children may not be able to repeat the words or spontaneously say rhyming words. They can benefit from hearing the nursery rhymes and your emphasis on the rhyming words. They can also experience the cadence of the rhymes and steady beat. To support your child's feeling of the beat, bounce your child on your knee or pat their back to the beat.

A New Favorite Book

Cost: Less than $10
Mess factor: None
Suggested location: A cozy spot

Experiences your children will have

- Looking at or pointing to familiar objects in photos
- Speaking one-, two-, or three-word statements about the photos
- Responding to an adult's statements

Materials

- Camera and digitally processed photos
- Heavy cardstock
- Adhesive tape or glue
- Hole puncher
- Fasteners (yarn, string, metal rings)
- Clear adhesive contact paper or a laminator for protecting photos (optional)

Before you get started:

1. Take and print pictures of important people (or pets) in your child's life as well as pictures of items that are familiar to your child (e.g., a stuffed animal). (The number of photos you use will be determined by your toddler's attention span; four or five pictures for younger toddlers and a larger selection for older toddlers.)
2. Cut the cardstock to the desired size — make the book larger to fit several pictures on a page or smaller to fit fewer pictures on a page. (With younger toddlers, put one or two pictures on each page.) Secure the pictures on to the pages with adhesive tape or glue, and use a hole puncher to create two or three holes that align on the left-hand side of each page. Secure the pages together with yarn, string, or metal rings.
3. Place a photo of your child (or children) on the front cover and write a title.

Beginning

Introduce the new book at a time when you typically read to your toddler.

Middle

Encourage your toddler to help you turn the pages or to hold the book independently. Give your child time to look at and respond to the pictures. Younger toddlers may simply point to pictures that catch their attention or might use a single word or gesture to label a picture they see. Older toddlers may label pictures, begin using two- and three-word phrases to talk about them, and respond to your statements or questions about the pictures.

End

As with so many activities for toddlers with varying attention spans and interests, you'll need to determine when your child is losing interest in looking at the book. If your child wants to continue to look at the book when it is time to move on, tell them that you'll look at it one more time before you put the book away. Assure your child that they can look at it again soon.

Cleanup

Let your child choose a special place to keep the book.

Younger children

Infants will also enjoy snuggling on your lap and gazing at the pictures. They will benefit from hearing your language as you label the pictures for them.

Older children

Older children will also enjoy a personalized book containing meaningful pictures of special people and objects. They might enjoy assisting you with choosing the pictures they want in their book, taking the pictures, and constructing the book. Writing each person's name underneath their picture or letting children write the person's name will add another dimension to the book as well.

Hints

- Instead of making your child a book, consider purchasing a small photo album with one or two photo sleeves per page that you can fill with pictures.

More!

If you and your children visit a zoo or farm, take pictures of the animals and use those to make another book.

Place photos of special people in magnetic picture frames on the lower half of your refrigerator so that toddlers can easily see them.

Special needs accommodations

To make turning pages easier for children who have motor delays, stick an adhesive dot of Velcro or felt on the top or bottom right-hand corner of each page in the book so the pages have more space between them and are easier to grab hold of.

Write Away

Cost: Under $5
Mess factor: Some
Suggested location: Kitchen or playroom

Experiences your children will have

- Making marks and scribbles
- Writing letterlike forms

Materials

- Washable markers or chubby crayons
- Paper
- Tape (optional)

Beginning

Cover your table (see "Hints" on the facing page), and make sure your child is safely seated. Place a piece of paper in front of your child (you can tape the paper onto the table so it doesn't slide). Let your child choose which color marker or crayon to use. (Toddlers often have more success with writing with a marker because they don't have to press as hard to make a mark.) If this is your child's first time using a writing tool, you may need to show them how to use the marker/crayon and help take the cap off of the marker (note that marker caps may be a choking hazard).

Middle

Younger toddlers may simply make random marks on their papers. While this might not seem significant, this exploratory stage is a very valuable step in their development of learning how to write. Keep in mind that it is common for toddlers to put items (e.g., crayons) in their mouths. If your child does this, offer a gentle reminder that crayons and markers are for writing on paper.

Demonstrate on your piece of paper how to make marks with a marker/crayon. Talk about what your child is doing, and use your own writing tool to imitate your child's actions.

End

When your child begins to lose interest, introduce a different color marker or crayon. If your child still seems uninterested, help your child down, and hang up your child's creations at toddler-height.

Cleanup

Wash your child's hands with warm, soapy water and wipe off their face and mouth with a warm washcloth to remove any marker smudges.

Younger children

To prepare infants' hands for a future of writing, give them lots of opportunities to practice grasping and holding objects (e.g., rattles, plush toys, stacking cups).

Older children

Expect to see older children writing letterlike forms and recognizable letters or numerals, especially if they have had plenty of practice using writing tools as toddlers. Give older children plenty of opportunities to practice writing by letting them make grocery lists, notes, cards, signs, and stories so they learn that that writing is much more than the rote practice of forming letters; it is a way of expressing themselves and a way of communicating with others.

Hints

- Consider purchasing a plastic tablecloth or shower curtain lining to place over your table for working on messy projects. Parents who cover their tables and are confident that their furniture is protected may feel more at ease letting their children explore art materials.
- Take this activity to a different level by taping a large sheet of butcher paper onto the floor of your kitchen (you may want to place the tablecloth or plastic lining underneath to protect your floor). Your toddlers might enjoy lying down on their stomach or sitting in the middle of the paper to write.

More!

Take this activity outside, and use crayons or sidewalk chalk for scribbling and writing on the sidewalk or driveway. Cleanup is as simple as washing toddlers' hands (and perhaps dusting off their pants). Children will enjoy seeing their writing displayed and will have a clean surface to repeat the activity after it rains!

Special needs accommodations

For toddlers with motor delays, consider purchasing a slant board (available from occupational therapy websites). Slant boards naturally place your child's wrist and hand in an optimal position for writing. Although a slant board may not be necessary to use when your child begins exploring writing tools, you may find it helpful as they become more interested in and purposeful about forming letters. You can also place a plastic needlepoint canvas sheet (available at most craft stores) underneath your toddler's piece of paper. Feeling the texture under the point of the marker or crayon while writing offers toddlers some sensory feedback.

3 Early Math and Discovery

Cool Tool

Cost: None
Mess factor: Some
Suggested location: For younger infants: wherever you nurse or give your infant a bottle; for older infants: kitchen (highchair)

Experiences your children will have

- Responding to an object
- Exploring a tool in their play

Materials

- Items for feeding (breast or bottle; infant spoon, bowl, and food)

Beginning

If you are nursing or feeding your infant a bottle, position yourself in a comfortable chair. If your infant is older and experienced at eating baby cereal or other types of food, secure your child in their highchair and sit in a nearby chair.

Middle

As you prepare to nurse or give your infant a bottle, notice how your infant responds by turning their head in the direction of the milk. Older infants will place their hand on your breast or reach both hands to hold on to the bottle.

For older infants, choose a spoon designed for infants. Infants may be a bit clumsy at getting the food to their mouth with a spoon; alleviate some of this frustration by feeding your hungry infant most of the food, before handing over the spoon. Place the spoon in your infant's hand, demonstrate how to scoop, guide the spoon and food to your child's mouth, and describe what you are doing. Then give your child a chance to use the spoon. Remember that your child might explore the spoon in different ways (e.g., put it in their mouth [without any food on it], throw it on the floor, or put it in their hair) without using it for its intended purpose. These are all normal ways that an infant explores an object. Describe what your child is doing (e.g., you might say, "You're using the spoon to pound on your tray").

If your infant's attempts to use the spoon aren't immediately successful, your child might simply pick up the pieces of food. If this happens, keep in mind that it takes young children time and experience to learn how to handle tools and for their muscles and coordination to develop enough to manipulate tools successfully. When your child is successful, encourage him or her (e.g., you might say, "You scooped up the carrots with the spoon and put them in your mouth!").

End

Your infant will eventually become full or tired of attempting to feed him- or herself. If your child is full, say that mealtime is all done. Otherwise, go ahead and finish the activity by feeding your child the rest of the meal.

Cleanup

Be prepared that you might have a messy infant to clean up! Use a washcloth to clean off your infant and the highchair tray and seat.

Older children

Older children will begin to use tools for their intended purpose and in ways that support their play (e.g., use markers, paper, and tape to make a birthday card or the end of a wooden spoon to get play dough out of a small container).

Hints

- Think about other tools younger infants might use to satisfy their needs or desires — a cold teething ring or a blanket, a stuffed animal, or other comfort item can all serve the purpose of providing comfort or stimulation.

More!

Give older infants new tools — that are safe — to explore. Here are some ideas of tools that infants might enjoy playing with:

In the kitchen

- Plastic bowls and lids
- Wire whisks, spatulas, large spoons
- Measuring cups and spoons
- Vegetable brush or pastry brush
- Pots, pans, metal baking pans

In the bathroom

- Hairbrush and comb
- Toothbrush
- Washcloths or towels

In the yard or sand box

- Shovel, hand rake, and bucket
- Watering can

At the kitchen table

- Crayons or markers
- Tape
- Wooden or plastic hammer or mallet (to use with play dough)
- Rolling pin (to use with play dough)

Special needs accommodations

Many adaptive tools are available to help children with special needs be successful (e.g., adapted or weighted spoons). Consult with an occupational therapist or search online for occupational therapy supplies to get some ideas for adaptive tools.

Exploring Objects

Cost: Less than $10 (depending on the materials used)
Mess factor: None
Suggested location: Anywhere

Experiences your children will have

- Looking at or handling one object and then another
- Gathering three or more objects

Materials

- Infant toys (choose toys that are easy to grasp, with bright colors, stimulating patterns, interesting textures, and soothing sounds)
- Safe and interesting objects found around your house that your infant can explore, such as basting brushes, whisks, or measuring spoons

Beginning

Depending on your child's age, position your infant on a blanket lying down, sitting in your lap, sitting on the floor with your support, or sitting independently. Surround your child with several interesting toys or objects, positioned nearby. (For younger infants, offer two or three objects; for older infants, increase to five or six objects.)

Middle

If your infant can't yet grasp objects, simply hold an interesting toy over their face to watch. An infant who can sit supported but can't grasp objects can watch toys that you hold in each of your hands. Give your child plenty of time to look at a toy and then shake the toy in your other hand.

If your infant can grasp objects and sit, either with your support or independently, give them a toy to hold and explore a toy. Younger infants may simply hold on to the toy with one hand, while older infants may transfer the toy from one hand to another. Present a new toy and observe what your child does (e.g., they might glance at the new toy but choose to continue exploring the first one or drop the first toy and grab the new one). Older infants will enjoy sitting on the floor with toys spread around them and may reach for and pick up two toys, one in each hand; exploring toys by looking first at one toy and then at the other; or placing one of the toys in their mouth, followed by the other one.

Older infants may start collecting toys and placing several in a pile. When children gather toys or objects in this way, you will know that they can attend to more than one object at a time, which is a milestone in their development.

End

Younger infants will show they are losing interest in this activity by crying, squirming, or arching their back. Try showing your child a new toy or changing their position before transitioning to a different activity. Older infants may show that they are finished by simply crawling away and finding something else to do. If your child is engaged in the activity but it's time to transition to another activity, try singing a cleanup song to let them know that it's time to put toys away and to indicate what's going to happen next.

Cleanup

An older infant may enjoy helping you clean up by transferring their collection into a box or basket. If your infant isn't enthusiastic about putting away the toys, consider letting him or her continue holding or exploring one toy or object as you move on to your next activity.

Older children

Older children will extend this activity by lining up the objects and noticing the properties of the objects in more detail (e.g., color, shape, size), which sets the stage for recognizing, copying, or extending simple patterns.

Hints

- As your child becomes more mobile, place toys, board books, and other easy-to-grasp objects around the room within your infant's reach. Have containers available, and demonstrate how to fill a container with toys. Your child may start using a container to hold objects he or she collects.

More!

Older children begin recognizing, copying, and extending simple patterns (e.g., blue-yellow-blue-yellow). While infants are still several developmental stages away from this milestone, introduce them to patterns through play and your daily routine. For example, lift your infant into the air while saying "Up" and then lower them while saying "Down." Repeat this several times while saying "Up...down...up... down" and continue until either your infant (or your arms!) get tired of this game.

Special needs accommodations

Infants with special needs can easily become overstimulated, especially when exploring something new or trying out a new skill. Minimize other distractions (e.g., lighting, background noise, and general visual clutter) before presenting your child with a new material or an idea. Speak in a calm tone, and offer gentle reassuring touches as your child explores a new toy or tries a new skill.

Do You See What I See?

Cost: None
Mess factor: None
Suggested location: Anywhere

Experiences your children will have

- Searching for objects in their immediate environment
- Naming objects

Materials

- None

Beginning

Tell your child that you are going to play a game where you have to hunt for things around the room: You are going to tell your child to hunt for something, and he or she is going to look for it. Start with objects that are big and easy to see. For example, you might say, "I spy a big, blue pillow." Encourage your child to point to or touch it.

Middle

For younger toddlers and for the first few rounds of play, keep the objects simple. Use the names of objects (e.g., *truck, pillow, bowl*) rather than descriptive words about the object (e.g., *red, bumpy, small*). If your child is struggling to find an object, give simple clues by pointing in the right direction or naming something that is near it. You can also collect a few items and encourage your child to locate an object from this small collection.

As your child becomes more familiar with the game and develops an increased vocabulary, increase the challenge by choosing objects that are partially out of sight (or out of sight but in a familiar place) or by giving descriptive words about the object (e.g., "It's something red that you put your head on when you go to sleep").

End

When you child begins to lose interest or it's time to move on to the next part of your day, let your child know that they can search for one more object and give them one to find (if you are short on time, make it something really obvious).

Alternatively, as you move to the next part of your day, ask your toddler to point out things along the way (e.g., you might say, "We have to go to the kitchen to make dinner. On our way, point to all the chairs you see").

Cleanup

None

Younger children

While they may not be able to find the objects the same way toddlers can, include younger children by pointing to and naming objects in their immediate environment. They can also share in the excitement when your toddler finds what he or she was looking for.

Older children

Include older children in the game by letting them pick the objects for your toddler to search for or having them search for their own (more challenging) objects. While keeping it simple for your toddlers, you can increase the challenge for older children by having them find objects whose names rhyme with a particular word, start with a certain letter, are bigger than a particular object, etc. Using these characteristics requires them to think about object and specific details.

Hints

- Keep it simple! Your child will enjoy playing when he or she is successful; increase the challenge as your child seems ready. If you offer something too difficult, reassure your child and offer a simpler object.

More!

Play this game as you are driving in the car, grocery shopping, or waiting in line as a fun way to pass the time as well as an opportunity for your child to find and name objects in unique environments.

Special needs accommodations

Use a few photos of familiar items you have around the house so children can see a picture of what they are looking for, rather than trying to hold an image in their mind.

A "Pairfect" Match

Cost: None
Mess factor: Minimal
Suggested location: Wherever you fold laundry

Experiences your children will have

- Matching socks based on color and other attributes
- Noticing similarities and differences

Materials

- Your family's socks

Beginning

Tell your child that you will need help with the laundry today. Put all the socks in one pile, and say something like "All of our socks are mixed up, and I need your help. Can you tell which of these socks belong together?"

Middle

Allow your child to closely examine the socks and hold them up together. Your child might find socks that match, socks that are the same color but a different length, socks that are the same length but a different color, or your child may simply play with the socks. Describe what your child is doing while identifying characteristics of the socks. For example, you might say, "You found two short white socks; that's a match!" or "You found a short black sock and a long black sock; I wonder if you can find two black socks that are both short" or "You're exploring the pile of socks. I see a red sock, a yellow sock, and a blue sock." Simply pointing out the socks' characteristics will increase your child's awareness of and vocabulary for similarities and differences.

End

After all the socks have been matched up or your child begins to lose interest, begin cleaning up and let your child know what will be happening next.

Cleanup

Gather up all the folded and unfolded laundry, and return it to the laundry basket or put it away.

Younger children

While they may not be able to recognize, identify, or match socks by color, younger children will enjoy "helping" you with the laundry and exploring the textures of the fabrics. Name and describe what they are feeling (e.g., "You're rubbing your fingers on that one; it's very smooth"). Offer your child simple things to "fold," such as washcloths or hand towels.

Older children

Offer older children more challenging tasks, such as sorting the laundry items by the person they belong to or where they need to be put away in the house. Encourage them to come up with their own ideas for how to sort the clothing.

Hints

- Socks are often folded by turning the ends into one of the socks, which requires a lot of coordination and dexterity. Your child might find it easier to simply fold the matching pair over or to lay one on top of the other.

More!

Children can also help sort the laundry before it goes into the washer, transfer laundry from the washer to the dryer, and remove items from the dryer. While it may take extra time, encouraging children's participation in household tasks makes it easier for you to get things done and meets children's desire to be close to you and learn from you.

Special needs accommodations

If your child cannot yet identify and distinguish characteristics of socks or other laundry, simply allow them to explore the textures. Be sure that you are folding laundry in a space your child has access to, such as a clean floor or a low couch, as this will make it easier for your child to join in.

A Walk in the Park

Cost: Less than $5
Mess factor: None
Suggested location: Outside at a local park

Experiences your children will have

- Exploring natural objects or materials
- Naming objects

Materials

- A large blanket (optional)
- A picnic lunch or snacks (optional)

Beginning

Find an area for you and your children to walk and explore (e.g., a paved pathway, an open grassy area, a short trail through the woods, or an area near a pond).

Middle

Plan for this activity to be a relaxed stroll, as naturally curious toddlers will enjoy finding objects to pick up and examine. As long as the objects of interest are safe, encourage your child to explore them. As your younger toddler does this, name the objects and briefly comment on them (e.g., "You found a rock. It looks heavy!").

Older toddlers may begin naming different objects they see. To try to understand the new things they are seeing, children add to their new experiences the knowledge they already have. For example, children might say "Doggy" when they see a squirrel. Understanding this part of toddlers' development will allow you to help your children make sense of the new information they are receiving. You might respond to your toddler with something like "It looks like a dog because it's running across the grass. That's called a squirrel." Expand your child's language and knowledge by adding more information, for example, "The squirrel is furry and has a long tail like our doggy at home, but he climbs trees…watch!"

End

Set up your lunch or snack (if part of your plan). As you enjoy your food, your child will continue to observe their natural surroundings. Make comments on what your child sees, names, or says. When you are finished, continue your walk in the park if your child is up for it; otherwise, pack up your things and head for home.

Cleanup

Your child can assist in cleanup by helping put items back in the picnic basket or bag, fold the blanket, and throw away the trash.

Younger children

Infants learn about nature by experiencing it — they feel the sunshine as it warms their bodies, the breeze blowing on their cheeks, and the soft blades of grass on their fingers or toes. Every sight, sound, and smell of nature that adults have grown accustomed to is a new sensory experience for an infant; take advantage of every opportunity to introduce your infant to the natural world.

Older children

With more developed language skills and a more sophisticated understanding of the natural world, older children will talk about where animals live and begin to notice changes in the natural environment. Simple comments and explanations from adults and from books will increase children's interest in the natural environment.

Hints

- Use extreme caution with young children around any kind of water; never leave them unattended near water. Also, keep in mind that some waterfowl can become aggressive and territorial. Keep your distance from them, and teach your children to be respectful of wild animals.

More!

When spring/summer rains come, dress yourself and your children in rain gear, grab the umbrella, and go outside. Point out the raindrops as they land in a puddle, look at the earthworms as they crawl across the sidewalk, let children feel the raindrops on their face, and encourage your toddlers to splash in a puddle or two!

If you live in a climate that is snowy in the winter and it's too cold to take children outside, bring the snow inside! Fill up buckets with freshly fallen snow, and transfer it into the kitchen sink or the bathtub. Put mittens on children's hands; gather a few measuring cups, spoons, and plastic bowls; and allow toddlers to explore.

Set out feeders for birds and squirrels in a space where toddlers can easily see them. Children will be fascinated as they watch the activities of the backyard wildlife.

Special needs accommodations

The outdoors is filled with a variety of sights, sounds, and smells, giving children who have visual or hearing impairments a wide range of sensory experiences. For children who are nonambulatory, call your local park district to find a list of parks that have paved pathways or trails available.

Counting Never Tasted So Good

Cost: None
Mess factor: Little
Suggested location: Kitchen

Experiences your children will have

- Indicating *more*
- Using a number word
- Counting by rote (saying numbers by memorization)
- Counting with one-to-one correspondence (developing a sense of number; touching each object and associating one number with each object counted)

Materials

- Finger foods (e.g., dry cereal; crackers; small pieces of fruit, vegetables, or meat)

Beginning

Place a small amount of food on your child's plate or highchair tray (keep more food on the table in a bowl/plate so children can see that there will be more available). Give your child time to pick up each piece of food and eat it. Talk about the food you've given your child, for example, "Your crackers are all gone!"

Middle

When their plate or tray is empty, young toddlers might indicate that they want more by reaching for the bowl or plate of food and/or by making a vocalization. Ask, "Do you want *more* bananas?" You may want to repeat the word *more* again and/or make the sign for *more* (look online for the American Sign Language image of how to sign *more*). Over time, if you repeat *more* to your toddler, you will find that they will begin saying or signing *more* when wanting more of something.

If your child has already moved beyond this developmental stage, count out loud (e.g., "1, 2, 3, 4, 5") when your toddler asks you for more of a food item as you place the items on their tray or plate. Over time, you will notice your child will begin using number words or start counting by rote; it's okay if he or she doesn't understand what each number means because experimentation with number words and rote counting is an important step in learning to count. Encourage your child's attempts at using number words and continue to model counting.

Older toddlers who have had practice saying number words will begin counting with one-to-one correspondence, starting with a just a few objects and gradually counting up to 10 or more objects.

End

This activity isn't meant to be a "counting drill and practice"; rather, it's meant to be an ongoing, natural process throughout mealtimes. The activity will draw to a close as the mealtime ends.

Cleanup

If your child enjoys their meal, there may be few edible "materials" to put away! Children may enjoy assisting in clearing or putting silverware into the dishwasher.

Younger children

Give your infant a single object to touch or handle (e.g., a rattle, bottle, teething ring) to teach your child the concept of *one*.

Older children

Older children will begin recognizing single-digit numbers. They will count to 10 and then beyond (using one-to-one correspondence) and will understand that the last number they count tells "how many."

Hints

- It's natural for children who are rote counting or counting with one-to-one correspondence to occasionally or consistently skip a number when counting (such as "1, 2, 4, 5, 6, 7") or repeat a number when counting (such as "1, 2, 3, 4, 4, 5, 6"). The most effective way to correct your beginning counter is to continue modeling by counting the numbers in the right order.
- When you finish counting a set of objects ("1, 2, 3, 4, 5, 6, 7, 8"), tell children how many you have when you are finished ("I have eight goldfish crackers!").

More!

Model *more* by saying or signing the word when your child wants more of a particular toy or item, another swing at the park, or another book to read.

To encourage your toddler to use number words or count by rote, count out loud when your toddler is climbing up steps or asking you to add blocks to their tower.

Have your child join you in counting with one-to-one correspondence (e.g., lining up three plastic bears and placing a marble by each).

Special needs accommodations

Frequently model the sign for *more* to help toddlers with developmental delays communicate *more*. Count with your toddler frequently, modeling the correct order of numbers, and encourage them to point to or touch each object as you count.

Kid Chef

Cost: Under $10
Mess factor: Little
Suggested location: Kitchen

Experiences your children will have

- Filling containers
- Nesting or stacking objects
- Using language to describe characteristics of objects

Materials

- Plastic bowls in at least three sizes
- A set of nesting cups or boxes ("nesting" toys fit inside one another in graduated order; provide your toddler with three or four nesting items to start with)
- A set or collection of one of the following: soft blocks, beanbags, sensory balls, snap-lock beads, plastic linking toys, lids from baby food jars
- Plastic or wooden spoons, plastic spatulas, measuring cups or spoons
- Pots and pans
- Empty food, condiment, or spice containers
- Containers to store items

Before you get started: Choose a low cabinet in your kitchen where you can see your child as you prepare meals but one that is far enough away from kitchen appliances and your workspace to keep your child safe. Replace the cabinet contents with some of the materials listed above. If applicable, remove the child-safety lock on the chosen cabinet. If there is no extra cabinet space in your kitchen, simply fill a plastic storage tub and place it on your kitchen floor.

Beginning

Show your toddler the new space when you have time to play together. Watch as your child dumps out, explores, fills, and fits together the toys and other materials, so you'll be able to support their play and learning.

Middle

If your child begins filling a container with materials, find some similar materials, fill your container, and describe what your child is doing. Continue to observe and imitate your child's actions and comment on what you see them do. If you frequently model measurement terms (e.g., *big, bigger, biggest*), you'll probably hear your child using some of these words as their vocabulary increases.

End

Give your toddler a large plastic or wooden spoon. If your child has filled a bowl with objects, suggest stirring the objects with the spoon or filling the spoon with some objects and transferring them to a different bowl.

Cleanup

As you begin cleaning up, fit many of the nesting objects together while leaving the largest and smallest ones on the floor and say something like, "I need two more cups. Can you find the little cup that fits in here? Now can you find the biggest cup?" (See "Hints" below for more cleanup ideas.)

Younger children

Place infants who can sit independently on a rug or blanket in a safe area of the kitchen. Put three or four nesting cups on the floor in front of them to play with and manipulate. For older infants, add a few objects that are the appropriate size to fit inside the cups.

Older children

Older children will use the same objects in a more purposeful way and perhaps use measurement terms while fitting items together. Consider adding collections of items for different measuring experiences (e.g., empty food boxes, spice containers).

Hints

- To make cleanup easier, place a label on the container that holds the collection of materials (i.e., a picture of the toy taped onto the container). Alternatively, tape one of the actual items (e.g., a baby food jar lid) onto the container.
- For younger toddlers, limit the number of materials in the cabinet. Too many items may be overwhelming to both you and your child, especially at cleanup time!

More!

Replace materials in the children's cabinet that have lost their intrigue with new materials. For example, replace the linking toys with sensory balls or baby-food jar lids or add pots and pans or empty food boxes/spice containers to the cabinet.

Special needs accommodations

Too many materials offered at one time may be overwhelming for children with special needs. Try giving your child three or four nesting cups and just one other set of materials for filling and emptying, or consider stocking the cabinet with some sensory toys (e.g., tactile sensory balls, spinners, twisty fidget toys).

4 Myself and Others

Emotions

Cost: None
Mess factor: None
Suggested location: Anywhere

Experiences your children will have

- Expressing emotions with their face and/or body
- Initiating physical contact with other people to express emotions

Materials

- Board books with photos of infants showing various emotions for the "More!" activity (next page)
- A mirror for the "More!" activity (next page)

Beginning

As you spend time with your infant, observe how your child communicates different emotions — by crying, tensing up, smiling, kicking their feet, babbling, laughing, or simply gazing contentedly. Older infants will begin initiating physical contact with others by kissing, patting, hugging, hitting, or even biting. How you respond to your child will depend on their needs, emotions, and developmental level.

Middle

When infants cry, they are typically communicating a need. Talk to your child and identify their emotions and needs (e.g., "You're so sad right now. You have such a hungry tummy"). In doing so, your child learns to be comforted by your voice and physical contact. When infants smile, they are communicating that they are happy and enjoy your company. Smile back, talk to, kiss, and gently touch your child to express that you enjoy their company too. As infants grow, so will their repertoire of emotional expression (e.g., fear, anger, amusement). Pay attention to the cues you receive, and continue doing whatever is amusing your child, or conversely, find a different toy, position/location, or activity if your child shows sign of disinterest.

Older infants will begin initiating physical contact with you and others. Some physical contact infants might initiate may not be pleasing; when your child bites you out of anger or frustration, you might feel shocked. It's important to calmly say to your infant something like "You're angry I took that away from you, but it's not safe to chew on." By responding this way, you're acknowledging your infant's anger, naming the emotion, and explaining the reason behind the emotion. This equips infants to deal with emotions in appropriate ways as they develop.

End

As you've probably already figured out, there really is no end to supporting children's emotions! The time you invest in responding to and supporting your infant's needs and emotions will be well worth your efforts as he or she grows.

Cleanup

None

Older children

As toddlers' language develops, they will begin using words that express basic emotions (e.g., *happy*, *sad*). Encourage toddlers' language and understanding of emotions by making comments (e.g., "Yes, she's happy") and perhaps even explain the reason for the emotion (e.g., "She is very happy; she sees her mom") to help your child begin to understand the reasons behind emotions.

Hints

- Be aware of your own emotions. Long nights with a crying infant can become very wearing. When you become frustrated, recognize your emotions and take a break (including a nap), if at all possible. If you don't have that kind of support, you may need to gently place your infant in a crib, step away for a brief moment, and calm yourself down before returning to care for your child.

More!

Your face (and the faces of other family members and primary caregivers) is the first and most important material your child will interact with, so allow plenty of time for your child to study (and touch) your face.

Find a cozy place for you and your child to look at a board book with pictures of babies expressing different emotions. Name the babies' different emotions so that your child can benefit from hearing a name given to each emotion.

Hold your child in front of a mirror and make faces at one another. Imitate the faces your child makes or play a game of peekaboo by moving yourself and your infant out of sight from the mirror and moving quickly back into sight. If your infant does not show interest in this game, return to the mirror a different day.

Special needs accommodations

Infants with limited mobility may be less able to position themselves to see your face, movements, and expressions. Be sure to position yourself so your child can see and study your face. Some infants may be easily startled or upset by too much activity near their face, or by loud noises or fast movements. If this is the case, enter your child's space slowly and calmly and pay attention to their cues.

Playing With the Piggies

Cost: None
Mess factor: None
Suggested location: Anywhere

Experiences your children will have

- Putting their fingers, thumbs, or foot in their own mouth
- Awareness of self by indicating something is theirs

Materials

- Hands, fingers, thumbs, feet, and toes

Beginning

Place your infant on their back (on a soft blanket on the floor, on a bed or changing table, or in a bouncy seat). An older infant can be sitting up (on the floor, in a highchair, or in the bathtub).

Middle

Lean in close, massage and kiss your infant's hands and feet, and say something like "I'm going to find your toes." If your child is wearing socks, pull them off, massage their feet a bit more, and give your child's toes a few more kisses. The tactile experience of having one's feet and toes exposed to the air, massaged, rubbed, and kissed could be an activity in itself, so give your child plenty of time to enjoy the experience before moving on.

Wriggle each toe on one foot (beginning with the big toe), and recite the nursery rhyme "This Little Piggy," moving to the next toe with each line of the rhyme:

> This little piggy went to market. This little piggy went home.
> This little piggy had roast beef. This little piggy had none.
> And this little piggy went *wee, wee, wee, wee* all the way home.

Traditionally, this nursery rhyme ends with adults tickling children's feet during the "wee, wee, wee, wee" part of the rhyme. In addition to tickling your child's foot while reciting that part of the rhyme, move your fingers up your child's legs and onto their stomach. Repeat the rhyme and activity on your child's other foot, and continue by alternating feet until your infant loses interest.

End

Your infant might indicate he or she is growing tired of the game by beginning to cry or squirm. Try massaging and kissing your child's feet again. Continue doing this if your child calms down and seems content. If your child continues to cry, take that as your cue that it's time to change their position or activity.

Older children

Older infants and toddlers continue to learn the concept of self by nonverbally indicating or verbally saying "Mine." For example, if a sibling attempts to take a favorite toy from their younger sibling, the younger child might turn away from the sibling and hold on tight to the object. As toddlers grow, they develop more of a sense of self. They show evidence of this by looking at themselves in the mirror and touching their face or body, or performing different actions and watching their reflection. They are also able to identify themselves in photos.

Hints

- In addition to tickling your infant, gently hold on to your child's feet and move their legs in a bicycle motion when you say "Wee, wee, wee, wee." You can also bring your infant's feet to his or her face as you say "Wee, wee, wee, wee."

More!

Older infants, who are beginning to understand more of your speech, may enjoy playing a game in which they anticipate getting tickled. When you have your child's attention, say "I'm going to get your piggies!" Slowly move toward your child's toes as you wriggle your fingers and repeat, "I'm going to get your toes!" Gently grab onto your child's toes and tickle their feet. As you move up your child's leg and to their stomach, say "I'm going to tickle your legs...I'm going to tickle your tummy!" If your child is amused by this game, continue playing together.

Bring your child's attention to their fingers by counting them. Wriggle each finger as you count, "One little finger, two little fingers, three little fingers..." You can also sing *"Ten Little Fingers"* as you touch or wriggle each finger.

Special needs accommodations

Infants with special needs may be more sensitive to tactile stimulation on their feet and toes. If your child becomes agitated when you touch their feet, find other places on your child's body that you can touch and massage. You might introduce your child's toes and feet to him or her by gently guiding the "little piggies" up to your child's mouth to explore.

So Close

Cost: None
Mess factor: None
Suggested location: Anywhere

Experiences your children will have

- Turning toward or away from objects or people
- Being persistent in moving toward things

Materials

- Interesting toys (with bright colors, stimulating patterns, interesting textures, and soothing sounds)
- Desirable objects (sippy cup, a favorite blankie, a pacifier)

Beginning

Observe which toys, objects, and sounds catch your child's attention (e.g., young infants might turn their head toward a bottle; older infants might reach for a brightly colored stuffed animal that jingles when shaken). Likewise, pay attention to objects, sounds, and other sensory input that your child might try to avoid (e.g., infants might turn their head away from a bright light).

Middle

If your infant is not yet mobile, try holding a colorful toy that makes a pleasing noise about 10–12 inches above your child's face (you'll know if your child can see and hear the toy because they may smile, coo, or kick their legs in excitement). Slowly move the toy from one side to the other (occasionally shaking it), and stop periodically to make sure your child is still tracking it.

If your infant is mobile, position an interesting toy near your child, making sure they know it's there. As your infant attempts to reach the toy, encourage your child by saying things like "Stretch just a little bit more!" or "You're going to get it!"

As infants grow, they are able to creep along the floor, sit independently, and move into a crawling position. At this stage, try positioning an interesting toy just beyond your child's reach. Over time, your child will begin to show more persistence in moving toward the object. Once your child reaches an object several times, you might want to position it a bit farther away. Be aware of children's reactions to this challenge, however, because they may become frustrated or may lose interest if the object seems too far away. To keep children interested in the challenge, be sure they experience frequent successes and encouragement.

Before you know it, your child will begin crawling, pulling to a standing position, cruising along furniture, and taking first steps. Infants' natural tendency to move toward interesting objects can become dangerous if the items of interest aren't child friendly or if dangerous obstacles are in the way; be sure to babyproof where necessary. You can also place interesting and infant-friendly toys and objects around your child's play space, which will encourage crawling and cruising.

End

Once infants reach the desired object, they may put it in their mouths; look at it; and feel, pat, or shake it. Your child may choose to continue playing with it or decide that the joy is in the "hunt" and look for another object to pursue!

Cleanup

Older infants can help put away toys by dropping items into a basket or box.

Older children

Older children will likely begin indicating their intentions by using language. They will begin with one or two words, such as "Up" and "Go night-night," and eventually use simple sentences, such as "I want to swing" or "Let's look for bugs."

Hints

- Eliminate distractions to infants' natural curiosity by turning off the television. The colors, movement, and noise created by the television may interrupt children's attempts to make contact with what they are trying to move toward.

More!

For older infants (eight to nine months), try hiding (or partially hiding) a favorite object underneath a blanket. Infants at this age are beginning to develop *object permanence*, which is an understanding that an object still exists even if it can't be seen. Infants who have not yet reached this developmental milestone may cry when a favorite object is covered (thinking that it is no longer there) or may find a different toy to pursue, which simply means that they aren't quite ready for this game. For infants who understand that the object or toy is still there even though they can't see it, hiding objects under a blanket becomes an amusing game.

Special needs accommodations

Infants with developmental delays may not gain mobility as quickly as their peers. In this case, encourage your child to move toward objects but understand that you may need to bring the objects to your child. Choose toys with interesting textures and bright colors that will be stimulating for your child.

It's a Date (A Playdate, That Is)

Cost: None
Mess factor: None
Suggested location: Anywhere

Experiences your children will have

- Watching, sharing objects with, and playing alongside other children
- Interacting with other children

Materials

- Favorite toys

Beginning

Find a comfortable place where the children can play together and where you and the other parent(s) can supervise and interact with them. Offer the children a variety of toys to play with. Children who have never played together before may be slow to interact with one another. Some children at this stage of development are content to simply play in the same space as other children or play with some of the same materials as others.

Middle

As children become comfortable in their surroundings, you may see the following natural behaviors:

- Children will watch each other.
- One child might offer a toy or show affection to another child.
- The children might play next to each other.
- Children might communicate with one another, using body language, words, phrases, or sentences, depending on their age and developmental abilities.

As your children play with one another, label what your children are doing, saying things like "Trevin, you're watching Bryce shake the rattle...the rattle makes a loud noise!" or "You're both very busy — Owen is playing with the cups and Ava is fitting the shapes into the shape sorter."

End

You may want to end your playdate with a healthy snack. While your toddlers are enjoying their snack, be sure to schedule their next playdate and determine where it will be.

Cleanup

Make cleanup simple for children. Encourage them to put their toys in a large play tub, toy chest, cabinet, or shelf.

Younger children

It's never too early to bring infants together to socialize; it gets really fun when babies are able to sit independently or move from a sitting to a crawling position!

Older children

Older children are typically more advanced in their social development and are more likely to play collaboratively with one another. When given the opportunity to play together, younger children can learn from their older peers, as the older children are typically more advanced in their language and social development.

Hints

- Having several of the same toy (or similar toys) is helpful in preventing social conflicts among toddlers.
- As your children spend time playing together, you will notice that they become more comfortable with each other. As time goes by, and your children grow and develop, they will begin to form genuine relationships.
- When mixing ages of children, be sure to keep a close watch on the toys they choose. Toys that are appropriate for preschoolers may be dangerous and pose choking hazards for infants and toddlers.
- Crowded play areas make it difficult to keep a watchful eye on toddlers. Toddlers may also become overstimulated in crowded spaces with multiple children present.

More!

Your children aren't the only ones who will benefit from playdates. Parents enjoy getting together and visiting with each other as well. It is good to nurture friendships with other parents, especially if the majority of your day is spent with young children; you may discover that you look forward to your children's playdate every bit as much as your children do!

Special needs accommodations

Offering children with special needs the opportunity to play and interact with their peers benefits all children. Children with special needs will benefit from watching their peers and how they play and speak. They may be motivated to attempt a new skill or play with a new toy after spending time watching their peers. Children without special needs will learn to be accepting of their peers as well as feel comfortable around children who might look or act differently than they do.

Just Another Ordinary Day

Cost: None
Mess factor: None
Suggested location: Anywhere

Experiences your children will have
- Indicating the end of an event
- Anticipating the next event in a familiar sequence

Materials
- Ordinary materials for your ordinary day
- Camera/photos for the "More!" activity (next page)

Beginning

Pay attention to natural routines that you've already established with your toddler (e.g., have dinner, take a bath, read a book before bed). Establishing a consistent yet flexible order of daily activities provides comfort, security, and a reassuring predictability for children. However, be cognizant of other events that might alter your routine (e.g., your child is interested in watching a garbage truck). These moments are filled with opportunities for language and learning so be sure to take advantage of them!

Middle

Once you've developed a routine that works, try to follow that routine consistently. Label each time of the day for your child (e.g., "It's lunchtime!"). When you follow a routine, you'll find that your child will begin to predict what part comes next. If you think that your toddler knows the sequence of your routine, ask them what comes next (e.g., "Bath is all done. Do you know what we're going to do next?").

End

Establish a routine for ending activities by giving a warning for cleanup time (e.g., singing a song to let your child know that cleanup time is approaching).

Cleanup

Make cleanup time a consistent part of your toddler's daily routine. Return toys and books to designated places, and consider placing pictures of children's toys on the baskets and shelves so they can see where to put their toys away.

Younger children

As infants develop, their involuntary reflexes become more voluntary movements. By engaging in voluntary actions (starting, stopping, and controlling their movements), infants begin to experience time intervals, an important developmental step.

Older children

Older children will begin to use sequence words such as *yesterday* and *tomorrow* correctly. They are also able to think back to events that happened several days, weeks, or months ago and to recall details of those personally meaningful experiences. Encourage older children to reflect and share those stories by engaging in conversations with them or by offering them paper and markers (or crayons) so they can draw pictures to show their experiences. After they finish illustrating, write down their words, creating a picture or book that depicts the special event.

Hints

- Life's necessities will impact your child's routine. Determine which part of your toddler's routine is the most flexible, and schedule your appointments, errands, or activities at that time. For many parents, skipping or delaying a toddler's naptime results in a tired and unhappy child, so try to plan accordingly.

More!

Take and print pictures of various times of the day (e.g., when your toddler gets dressed, eats breakfast, goes for a walk). Hang those pictures on a door or a small, portable bulletin board in the order in which they happen. When an activity is finished, point to the appropriate picture and say something like "We're all done with breakfast. Now it's time to go outside for a walk." By using this type of visual reminder, toddlers will be more likely to predict the next activity.

Special needs accommodations

Some children with special needs experience anxiety when their routine is disturbed and may benefit from simple "first/then" charts to help them understand a change in their routine. To make a "first/then" chart to illustrate, for example, that your child is going to have a diaper change before going outside, draw a line down the middle of a piece of paper and write *first* on one side of the line and *then* on the other side. Find photographs for illustrations, such as those of a diaper and one of outside, and place them in the appropriate spaces on the chart.

Thinking Backwards

Cost: None
Mess factor: None
Suggested location: Anywhere

Experiences your children will have

- Returning to an object of interest
- Pointing to or showing something they played with
- Saying one thing he or she did soon after the event

Materials

- New or favorite toys or objects

Beginning

As you and your children play together, pay attention to what toy or object they favor and what they do with it. Gathering information like this will help you support your toddlers as they begin to develop the ability to form and hold images in their mind.

Middle

Call attention to your toddler's developing ability to remember where something of interest is located. For example, when your child returns to a sippy cup, you might say, "You left your sippy cup on the couch before naptime. You remembered where it was!" Older toddlers may point to or show you something they played with, and, eventually, will be able to tell you something they did soon after the event has taken place. To support these developing skills, talk to your toddlers as they play, imitate their actions, and comment on what you are each doing.

Cleanup

Because toddlers are learning to remember where objects are located, store your children's toys and books in a consistent place. Consider placing pictures of your children's toys on the baskets and shelves so their toys are always put away in the same place — it will be easier for them to clean up if they can match the toys to the pictures. As you clean up, give your child a book and ask, "Do you know where this book goes?" Encourage your child's ability to recall by saying something like "You played with a lot of toys today, but you really enjoyed building with your blocks" as you help children put the blocks back on the toy shelf.

End

After you clean up, say something like "You had fun building with something on the floor. Do you remember what you were playing with?" Children might respond by pointing to something they played with or bringing you a block. Respond by saying something like "I remember you played with the blocks. We stacked them high!"

Younger children

Infants are not yet able to form mental images of events but will respond positively to pleasurable events, as if to say, "I'd like you to do that again!"

Older children

Older children who have had practice reflecting on their experiences will move to the next developmental stage, in which they are able to think and talk about several things at once. Encourage children to expand on what they share by asking more questions, such as "What else did you do?" and "What happened after that?"

Hints

- Depending on children's level of development, they may not respond to questions about what they played with. Consider giving a clue (e.g., you might say, "After you stacked them, you kicked them and they fell down. Can you show me what you were playing with?"). You may realize (after a couple of tries) that your child has not yet reached the stage of being able to point to or talk about what they played with; remember that each child develops at their own pace.
- Often, young children will remember the very last thing they did, which is easier for them to remember than the event in which they spent the most time. Even if you have a specific idea in mind about what your toddler should remember, your child might still choose to show or talk to you about the last thing they did.
- Make comments and ask questions about an activity shortly after it occurs; beginning recallers are more likely to remember events that have just happened.

More!

Use a cloth bag to collect a few toys that older toddlers played with. Soon after you finish playing, pull the objects out of the bag one at a time and talk about what children did with each of the objects. (*Note:* If your toddler prefers to continue playing with the object, let your child play and try this idea on another day.)

Special needs accommodations

Children with special needs might need extra visual prompts to help them remember what they did. Take pictures or video of your older toddler playing throughout the day. Talk with or for your child, describing details of the play materials and what he or she did while playing.

5 Physical Development and Healthy Habits

Pick It Up

Cost: Less than $10 per toy
Mess factor: None
Suggested location: Anywhere

Experiences your children will have

- Opening and closing their hands
- Using small muscles to handle or pick up objects

Materials

- Infant toys (choose toys that are easy to grasp and with bright colors, stimulating patterns, interesting textures, and soothing sounds)
- Safe and interesting objects (a clean hairbrush, recycled yogurt container, kitchen spatula, plastic water bottle)
- Age-appropriate finger foods

Beginning

Observe how your child uses their hands and fingers. Note that your child's ability to handle toys depends on their age, developmental level, and prior experiences.

Middle

Offer your child one or two objects to hold (too many choices can be overwhelming), understanding that they may only hold the object for a short time before letting it fall. Be sure to give the object back to your child to let them try to hold it again.

With practice, children will begin grasping objects with their whole hand for longer time periods. As children develop, they'll be able to reach for a toy, pick it up, bring it to their mouth, and then transfer a toy from one hand to the other. Many infants like to drop an object from a highchair on to the floor, look at it, and wait for an adult to pick it up. Play this game with your child (although you may quickly grow tired of it!), because it is an important part of your child's development and gives them invaluable opportunities to practice grasping and handling objects.

As infants develop, they'll be able to pick up smaller objects, first by sliding their thumb to the side of their index finger and later by using their thumb and finger in a pincer grasp. This skill often develops at about the same time children are ready to eat finger food. Offer children small amounts of finger food so they aren't tempted to put too much food in their mouth at one time. Although it may be tempting to feed infants yourself to avoid messes, let them feed themselves finger foods so they can develop their fine-motor skills.

End

Younger infants will stay interested in activities for much shorter periods of time than will older infants. You'll know it's time to find a different toy (or even perhaps an entirely different activity) when they look away from the toy, show no interest in attempting to grasp or hold the object, or move away to find something else.

Cleanup

Encourage older infants to help you pick up an object and drop it in a box or basket when it's time to put toys away.

Older children

Toddlers will begin fitting materials together and taking them apart. Offer toddlers toys such as interlocking blocks, pop beads, or nesting cups, which encourage them to fit materials together and then take them apart.

Hints

- As your infant becomes more mobile and able to pick up small objects, be sure that objects that could pose a choking hazard are out of their reach. If there are older children in the home, keep their age-appropriate toys (with small pieces) in a room separate from the rooms where your infant is able to crawl and cruise.

More!

Infants enjoy toys that make noise by shaking, pounding, and dropping them. If your infant enjoys pounding or banging objects, offer items such as a light-weight wooden or plastic hammer or mallet and something safe on which to pound.

Consider introducing homemade play dough (you can find a recipe online) to your children, but keep in mind that the play dough may go straight into their mouths! If your child has never experienced play dough, show them how to poke or squeeze it. Pick off small pieces, and encourage your child to do the same. Offer your child a light-weight wooden or plastic hammer or mallet for pounding the play dough or a collection of smaller objects (such as pegs or plastic people) to pick up and poke into the play dough.

Special needs accommodations

Parents of children with developmental delays must keep in mind that it may take longer before their infants are able to grasp toys and pick up small objects. Continue to offer infants opportunities to explore and manipulate interesting infant toys and other materials, knowing that children will reach the developmental milestones in their own time.

Kick It

Cost: None
Mess factor: None
Suggested location: Living room or other comfortable space

Experiences your children will have

- Stretching their leg muscles and kicking their feet
- Cause and effect — moving their bodies and causing objects to move

Materials

- For nonmobile infants: an open space and a fixed, soft surface, such as a couch
- For nonmobile or newly mobile infants: ribbons or small blanket
- For sitting, crawling, and walking infants: soft balls that your infant can kick or throw

Beginning

For nonmobile infants: With your infant sitting up or lying down, touch the bottom of your child's feet with the palms of your hands. This will likely result in your child pushing against or kicking your hands.

For mobile infants: Choose a space where your infant has room to move, and offer some balls to kick. Accept that your child might instead choose to throw the balls.

Middle

Describe your infant's actions. For example, you might say something like, "You're kicking against my hands! Kick, kick!"

For nonmobile infants: Repeat this activity with your infant's feet up against a sturdy, padded piece of furniture (e.g., a couch). You can also dangle ribbons or a small blanket near your child's feet for them to kick. Infants will enjoy watching the way the ribbons move and feel them against their feet as they kick. This increases children's awareness of their bodies and different ways they can use them.

For mobile infants: Comment on how your child chooses to use the balls, and use them in the same way. Describe how your child is moving their body and the effect those movements have on the ball. For example, you might say, "You swung your leg back and kicked the ball. It rolled all the way over under the window" or "You held the ball in both hands and threw it way up." These comments increase children's awareness of their bodies and the different ways they can use them.

End

Let your infant know that it is almost time for the next part of the day by telling them what is coming up next. After your child has kicked a few more times or has lost interest, gently pick up your infant and prepare for the next part of your day.

Cleanup

Gather up any materials you have used and set them aside for use at another time.

Older children

Older children may enjoy kicking balls and trying out different ways to use their bodies. Assist them in finding soft balls and a space where young infants will not be bumped, trampled, or startled. Older siblings of sitting, crawling, or walking infants may enjoy gently rolling or kicking a ball back and forth with their younger sibling.

Hints

- Your infant will stay engaged with activities longer when you are present and are reflecting their emotions. Be sure to stay on your child's level, make eye contact, offer gentle touches, and periodically make comments about how your child is moving.

More!

Throughout the day, comment on your child's use of their body (e.g., moving arms or legs, moving in different ways, moving different body parts at the same time). Encouraging children to move their bodies in different ways will help strengthen their muscles for future tasks such as walking, running, jumping, and climbing.

Special needs accommodations

Be sure to position children in ways that are comfortable while allowing them to explore ways to move their bodies. Placing nonmobile infants on their back is usually a comfortable position for making eye contact and moving arms or legs freely. If you have questions or concerns about your child's physical development, contact your pediatrician.

Follow the Leader

Cost: None
Mess factor: None
Suggested location: A large, open space

Experiences your children will have

- Trying out different physical movements
- Making suggestions to others about how to move
- Copying the ideas of others

Materials

- None

Beginning

Start the activity by singing a simple, familiar song or use a familiar tune and sing something like this (to the tune of "Row, Row, Row Your Boat"):

> March, march, march your feet as we sing this song.
> March, march, march your feet as we sing this song.

March your feet as you sing.

Middle

Ask your child to show you (if nonverbal) or tell you (if verbal) another way to move. Give your child time to think, decide, and display a movement and then copy and name their idea (e.g., "You're wiggling your hips"). Continue to sing the song from the beginning by changing the words to match the actions (e.g., "Wiggle, wiggle, wiggle your hips as we sing this song") or simply copy your child's movement. Try out several ideas, ask your child for input, and offer other suggestions of ways to move.

Do this activity in one place (e.g., marching in one place), or, alternatively, move around an open space (e.g., marching around in a circle).

End

When your child begins to lose interest or you need to move on to the next part of your day, let your child try one more idea that you do together before letting them know what will be happening next.

You can also encourage your child to choose a way to move to the next part of your day. For example, if you need to go to the bus stop to pick up an older child, you might say, "We need to go to the bus stop to pick up Marcus. How should we move our bodies to get there?" Use your child's idea as the way to get there.

Cleanup

None

Younger children

Carry nonmobile children in your arms or in a sling or carrier during this activity. For mobile children, encourage them to join in by crawling or scooting along. Be sure to move at a slow pace so they can keep up with you, and avoid dangerous obstacles (e.g., stairs).

Older children

Encourage older children to join in and try out the ideas suggested by your toddler. Be sure to give older children a turn to be leaders too. They can suggest ideas for the rest of the family to copy.

Hints

- As you offer ideas for your child to try, keep it simple and avoid complex movements, such as skipping and doing jumping jacks. If children are not able to copy your ideas, they may feel discouraged and quickly give up.

More!

Use this activity as a fun way to transition, such as going from the dinner table to the bathroom or going out to the car. Using this as a transition activity can reinforce children's learning and also make the transition easier because children are having fun while leading a task.

Special needs accommodations

For children that are not yet mobile or use a device to move around, play follow the leader in a stationary spot. Focus on copying and initiating movements that your child is able to do, such as kicking up a leg, waving arms, or bending and straightening. This allows for exploration of their motor skills as well as the social experience of copying and imitating.

Splishy, Splashy, Wishy, Washy

Cost: None
Mess factor: Some
Suggested location: Kitchen or bathroom

Experiences your children will have

- Learning the steps of hand washing
- Exploring water and soap

Materials

- Sink (if the sink is high, provide a stool on a nonslip rug so your child can reach)
- Running water
- Soap
- Towel for drying
- Camera and printed pictures for the "More!" activity (next page)

Beginning

Invite your child to the sink and let them know that you are going to explore water and practice hand washing. If a stool is needed, help your child up onto the stool and turn on cool or lukewarm water. **Be sure to always closely supervise children standing on stools and using water.**

Middle

Allow your child time to explore the running water, and comment on your child's actions and reactions, for example, "You're letting the water run over your fingers." Explain to your child that after eating, bodily care, or playing outside, it is important to wash hands to get rid of any germs.

Let your child know that the first step in hand washing is getting their hands wet, and then offer your child soap. Encourage your child to rub their hands around to make bubbles. This step is important because the bubbles capture and carry away the germs; it is recommended to scrub hands with bubbles for 60 seconds. Help your child get used to this length of time by singing a favorite song or two while your child scrubs. Sing slowly, and ask your child to scrub until the song is over. Next, encourage your child to rinse their hands off in the stream of water. Allow your child to repeat the steps of hand washing again if interested.

COR Advantage item: K. Personal care and healthy behavior

End

Let your child know that there are two minutes left to wash hands and explore the water. After two minutes, assist your child in turning off the water and cleaning up.

Cleanup

Dry off your child's hands, and wipe any water that has splashed onto the counter or floor around the sink.

Younger children

Young children will also enjoy splashing in the water. If they cannot stand up at a sink on a stool, help them by holding them up or placing a small tub of water on the floor or on a highchair tray where they can reach. Be sure to supervise children using water at all times.

Older children

Older children will be able to stand independently and remember all the steps of hand washing. They can also pump the soap and wash other parts of their body, such as their faces. They may enjoy reminding younger children of what step is next and can help pump the soap or wipe up any splashed water.

Hints

- Give children time to explore the water as it is a new, interesting sensation for them and encourage them to take their time when washing their hands.

More!

To support your child's understanding and memory of the steps of hand washing, take a picture of each step, print it, and display the pictures above or near the sink as a reference. This will increase children's independence in hand washing and help ensure that they complete each step.

Special needs accommodations

If children cannot stand up at a sink on a stool, help them by holding them up or placing a small tub of water on the floor or on a highchair tray where they can reach. Children who are resistant to putting their hands or bodies in water can experience washing up by using a damp washcloth, then a soapy one, and finally a damp washcloth to rinse. If they are curious about the water but don't want to touch it, offer a washcloth for dipping or a toy (e.g., a pitcher with a handle) to explore the water so that they can become comfortable with it.

Poke, Pull, Squish

Cost: Under $5
Mess factor: Some
Suggested location: Kitchen

Experiences your children will have

- Using the small muscles in their hands and fingers
- Hearing new vocabulary words

Materials

- Homemade play dough (softer in consistency than store-bought dough)
- Items for poking into the play dough (plastic pegs, plastic animals or people figures, Popsicle sticks)
- Items for pounding the play dough (lightweight wooden/plastic hammers)
- Items for filling (plastic cups or bowls)

Beginning

Give your toddler time to explore a mound of play dough. Imitate your child's actions, and introduce new vocabulary words to describe what your child is doing or experiencing (e.g., *squishy, poke, flat, heavy,* and *salty*).

Middle

Observe how your child plays with the dough. If your child pokes it, offer other items that are good for poking (e.g., Popsicle sticks, plastic pegs). If your child pulls it apart, provide a plastic bowl or cup to fill with play dough pieces. If your child pounds the dough, offer a lightweight wooden/plastic hammer. Use your mound of play dough and other materials in the same way your child is using them and describe what you are doing.

Homemade Play Dough

Materials

- 1 cup water
- 1 tbsp. vegetable oil
- ½ cup salt
- 1 tbsp. cream of tartar
- Food coloring
- 1 cup flour
- Parchment or wax paper

Directions

1. Combine in a pot the water, oil, salt, cream of tartar (so dough will last for six months), and food coloring (start with a few drops and add more as needed), and heat until warm.
2. Remove from heat and add the flour.
3. Stir and knead until smooth. (Knead the dough on wax/parchment paper until it begins to cool to keep the hot dough from sticking.)
4. Store dough in an airtight container or a plastic freezer bag.

End

Depending on children's interest, this activity might last a short or a long time. Follow their lead, and end the activity when they begin to lose interest.

Cleanup

Let your toddler know that it's almost time to put the play dough away. You might want to sing a cleanup song (singing a cleanup song gives your child a warning that the activity is almost over). Encourage your child to put the play dough back in the container, and then give them a wet rag to help you wipe the table.

Younger children

Expect younger children to simply explore the properties of play dough by poking, pulling, pounding, and squeezing; these experiences serve to strengthen the small muscles in children's hands as they play.

Older children

Older children can help you make the play dough by adding the ingredients, stirring the mixture, or kneading the cooled play dough.

Because older children can manipulate objects with more dexterity and precision, offer them tools such as rolling pins, cookie cutters, garlic presses, or scissors.

Hints

- Remember, at this age, children are exploring the dough and how to manipulate it rather than making something recognizable or intentional.
- Squeezing, kneading, and pulling apart play dough strengthens the small muscles in toddlers' hands. Helping toddlers develop strength and control in their fingers now will prepare them for handling writing tools and participating in other fine-motor activities (such as cutting with scissors or zipping their coat).

More!

Add bowls, muffin tins, and other cooking and baking utensils so that children can fill and empty the bowls and other containers with their play dough pieces.

Special needs accommodations

Children with special needs may be sensitive to new smells or to the way things feel in their hands. If your child reacts to play dough in a negative way, don't worry. There are many other ways to strengthen the small muscles in your child's hands (e.g., providing them with balls that light up when they are squeezed). Giving your toddler ample opportunities to manipulate a variety of objects (starting with chubby objects that are easy to hold) will help develop their fine-motor skills.

Appendixes

Appendix A: HighScope Infant-Toddler Key Developmental Indicators (KDIs)

A. Approaches to Learning

1. **Initiative:** Children express initiative.
2. **Problem solving:** Children solve problems encountered in exploration and play.
3. **Self-help:** Children do things for themselves.

B. Social and Emotional Development

4. **Distinguishing self and others:** Children distinguish themselves from others.
5. **Attachment:** Children form an attachment to a primary caregiver.
6. **Relationships with adults:** Children build relationships with other adults.
7. **Relationships with peers:** Children build relationships with peers.
8. **Emotions:** Children express emotions.
9. **Empathy:** Children show empathy toward the feelings and needs of others.
10. **Playing with others:** Children play with others.
11. **Group participation:** Children participate in group routines.

C. Physical Development and Health

12. **Moving parts of the body:** Children move parts of the body (turning head, grasping, kicking).
13. **Moving the whole body:** Children move the whole body (rolling, crawling, cruising, walking, running, balancing).
14. **Moving with objects:** Children move with objects.
15. **Steady beat:** Children feel and experience steady beat.

D. Communication, Language, and Literacy

16. **Listening and responding:** Children listen and respond.
17. **Nonverbal communication:** Children communicate nonverbally.
18. **Two-way communication:** Children participate in two-way communication.
19. **Speaking:** Children speak.
20. **Exploring print:** Children explore picture books and magazines.
21. **Enjoying language:** Children enjoy stories, rhymes, and songs.

E. Cognitive Development

22. **Exploring objects:** Children explore objects with their hands, feet, mouth, eyes, ears, and nose.
23. **Object permanence:** Children discover object permanence.
24. **Exploring same and different:** Children explore and notice how things are the same or different.
25. **Exploring more:** Children experience "more."
26. **One-to-one correspondence:** Children experience one-to-one correspondence.
27. **Number:** Children experience the number of things.
28. **Locating objects:** Children explore and notice the location of objects.
29. **Filling and emptying:** Children fill and empty, put in and take out.
30. **Taking apart and putting together:** Children take things apart and fit them together.
31. **Seeing from different viewpoints:** Children observe people and things from various perspectives.
32. **Anticipating events:** Children anticipate familiar events.
33. **Time intervals:** Children notice the beginning and ending of time intervals.
34. **Speed:** Children experience "fast" and "slow."
35. **Cause and effect:** Children repeat an action to make something happen again, experience cause and effect.

F. Creative Arts

36. **Imitating and pretending:** Children imitate and pretend.
37. **Exploring art materials:** Children explore building and art materials.
38. **Identifying visual images:** Children respond to and identify pictures and photographs.
39. **Listening to music:** Children listen to music.
40. **Responding to music:** Children respond to music.
41. **Sounds:** Children explore and imitate sounds.
42. **Vocal pitch:** Children explore vocal pitch sounds.

Appendix B: COR Advantage Items

Approaches to Learning

A. Initiative and planning
B. Problem solving with materials
C. Reflection

Social and Emotional Development

D. Emotions
E. Building relationships with adults
F. Building relationships with other children
G. Community
H. Conflict resolution

Physical Development and Health

I. Gross-motor skills
J. Fine-motor skills
K. Personal care and healthy behavior

Language, Literacy, and Communication

L. Speaking
M. Listening and comprehension
N. Phonological awareness
O. Alphabet knowledge
P. Reading
Q. Book enjoyment and knowledge
R. Writing

Mathematics

S. Number and counting
T. Geometry: Shapes and spatial awareness
U. Measurement
V. Patterns
W. Data analysis

Creative Arts

X. Art
Y. Music
Z. Movement
AA. Pretend play

Science and Technology

BB. Observing and classifying
CC. Experimenting, predicting, and drawing conclusions
DD. Natural and physical world
EE. Tools and technology

Social Studies

FF. Knowledge of self and others
GG. Geography
HH. History

English Language Learning (ELL)

II. Listening to and understanding English
JJ. Speaking English

Appendix C: Recipes and How-to Instructions

Homemade Bath Paint

Materials

- ¼ cup tear-free baby wash or shampoo
- ¼ cup corn starch
- 1–2 tbsp. water
- 3–4 drops food coloring

Directions

1. Combine cornstarch, shampoo, and food coloring.
2. Add water, a little bit at a time, until the mixture reaches the desired consistency. If it gets too runny, add more cornstarch; if it gets too thick, add more water.
3. Store paint in small plastic containers (with lids).

Homemade Play Dough

Materials

- 1 cup water
- 1 tbsp. vegetable oil
- ½ cup salt
- 1 tbsp. cream of tartar
- Food coloring
- 1 cup flour
- Parchment or wax paper

Directions

1. Combine the water, oil, salt, cream of tartar (ensures that dough will last for six months), and food coloring (start with a few drops and add more to get desired color) in a pot, and heat until warm.
2. Remove from heat and add the flour.
3. Stir and knead until smooth. (*Note:* Knead the dough on wax or parchment paper until it begins to cool to keep the hot dough from sticking to your fingers.)
4. Store dough in an airtight container or a plastic freezer bag.

Homemade Shakers

Materials

- Plastic eggs
- Empty plastic spice jars
- Empty formula bottles
- Empty plastic baby food containers
- Empty travel shampoo containers
- Empty water bottles (8 oz. size)
- Glue and/or tape

Directions

1. Choose several of the containers listed in Materials (above) to make shakers of different sizes, weights, and sounds.
2. Fill each container with one of the following contents (choose one per container):
   - Pea gravel
   - Fish tank gravel
   - Pennies
   - Sand
   - Beads
   - Rice
   - Dried beans
   - Screws or nails

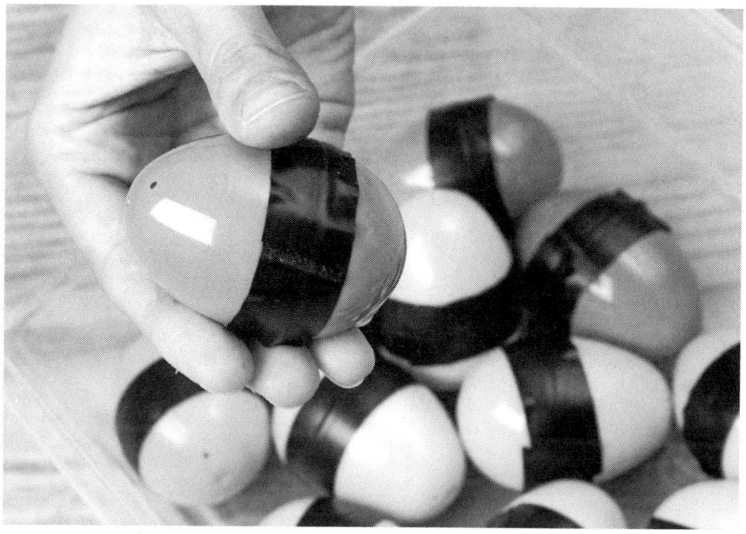

3. Securely seal the container with glue and/or tape.
4. Be sure to use supervision when giving these shakers to young children to ensure that materials in shakers don't come out.

Homemade Textured Board Book

Materials

- Scraps of cloth such as felt, satin, or velvet
- Fabric tassels, trims, and fringe
- A piece of sandpaper
- Ribbons
- Heavy cardstock
- Scissors
- Hole puncher
- Glue

Directions

1. Cut square sheets of heavy cardstock, paper, or cardboard into pieces about 6" x 6" (or whatever size you prefer).
2. Cut scraps of cloth and other textured items into pieces that will fit onto each page.
3. Secure the items onto pages with glue, leaving enough room on the left side of each page for holes and fasteners.
4. Punch two or three holes on the left side of each page (be sure the holes on each page line up with each other).
5. Use ribbons to secure the pages.

Homemade Picture Book

Materials

- Camera (a camera on a smart phone will work too) and digitally processed photos
- Heavy cardstock
- Adhesive tape or glue
- Hole puncher
- Fasteners (yarn, string, metal rings)
- Clear adhesive contact paper or a laminator for protecting photos (optional)

Directions

1. Use a camera to take pictures of important people (or pets) in your child's life as well as pictures of items that are familiar to your child (e.g., a favorite stuffed animal or blanket, a favorite food, your child's bed).
2. Once you have a selection of photos that you've printed, you are ready to make the book. (The number of photos you use will be determined by your toddler's attention span; younger toddlers may only sit to look at four or five pictures, while older toddlers may enjoy looking at a much larger selection of pictures.)
3. Cut the cardstock to the desired size — make the book larger to fit several pictures on a page or smaller to fit fewer pictures on a page. (With younger toddlers, you may want to put just one or two pictures on each page.)
4. Secure the pictures on to the pages with adhesive tape or glue.
5. Use a hole puncher to create two or three holes on the left-hand side of each page. Make sure the holes line up in the same place for each page of the book.
6. Secure the pages together with yarn, string, or metal rings.
7. Place a photo of your child (or children) on the front cover and write a title above or below the picture.

About the Authors

Nancy Vogel

Nancy Vogel has taught in a number of early childhood settings over the past 25 years, including HighScope's Demonstration Preschool, state-funded preschools, early childhood special education programs, and kindergarten programs. In addition, she has worked as a HighScope Field Consultant and Trainer. She is the author of *Setting Up the Preschool Classroom* (2009), *Making the Most of Plan-Do-Review* (2001), many of the *You and Your Child* parent newsletters (2001), and *Getting Started: Materials and Equipment for Activing Learning Preschools* (1997). She earned a degree in early childhood education and special education from Bradley University in Peoria, Illinois.

Nancy lives in Metamora, Illinois, with her husband, Curt, and their three teenage children, Ruth, Samuel, and Luke. She serves as Director of Children and Family Ministries at St. Mark's Lutheran Church, in Washington, Illinois.

Christine Snyder

Christine Snyder is an Early Childhood Specialist at the HighScope Educational Research Foundation and a certified HighScope teacher and trainer. She taught for two years in the HighScope Demonstration Preschool and currently focuses on teacher training and developing curriculum materials for infant- toddler and preschool programs. Christine has facilitated training throughout the United States as well as internationally. In addition to face-to-face training, she also develops and conducts online training. She is the author of the infant and toddler versions of *Lesson Plans for a Strong Start: The First 30 Days* as well as several articles in *Extensions* and *ReSource*. In addition, Christine has contributed to the production of web-based training clips and other classroom resources for teachers.

Christine has worked in the early childhood education field since 1998 in a variety of roles: infant-toddler teacher, preschool teacher, before/after school teacher, center director, and teacher trainer/mentor. During her time as a center director, she led her program through the National Association for the Education of Young Children (NAEYC) accreditation process.

Christine is an associate professor at Madonna University in Livonia, Michigan. In addition, she serves on the NAEYC Council for Accreditation and the MiAEYC Nominations Committee as well as the education advisory councils for Eastern Michigan University, Madonna University, and Washtenaw Community College.